The Aristocratic Temper
of Greek Civilization

The Aristocratic Temper
of Greek Civilization

Chester G. Starr

New York   Oxford
OXFORD UNIVERSITY PRESS
1992

Oxford University Press

Oxford   New York   Toronto
Delhi   Bombay   Calcutta   Madras   Karachi
Kuala Lumpur   Singapore   Hong Kong   Tokyo
Nairobi   Dar es Salaam   Cape Town
Melbourne   Auckland

and associated companies in
Berlin   Ibadan

Published by Oxford University Press, Inc.
200 Madison Avenue, New York, New York 10016

Oxford is a registered trademark of Oxford University Press

Library of Congress Cataloging-in-Publication Data
Starr, Chester G., 1914–
The aristocratic temper of Greek civilization /
Chester G. Starr.
p. cm.   Includes bibliographical references and index.
ISBN 0-19-507458-0—ISBN 0-19-507459-9 (pbk.)
1. Nobility—Greece—History. I. Title.
HT653.GS75 1992
305.5'223'09495—dc20   91-30822

2 4 6 8 9 7 5 3 1
Printed in the United States of America
on acid-free paper

To
Pansie and Ernie Dawn
in memory of Tehran
and also to Zabah, who saved our lives

Preface

For a number of years the role of aristocrats in ancient Greece has been on my mind, partly because I judge that their place has been generally misconceived, an interesting product of modern prejudices. The present work is an effort to redress the balance. One must use Greek terms such as *arete* on occasion, which are not always easily translated, but I have sought to suggest reasonable approximations.

I am much indebted to the counsel of two of my former students, Arther Ferrill of the University of Washington and Josiah Ober of Princeton University and to the careful scrutiny by two referees. But above all, as usually, I owe much to the keen eye and firm criticism of my wife Gretchen. If my books can be considered readable, this is the fruit of her thoughtful attention.

Ann Arbor   *Chester G. Starr*
September 1991

Contents

The Aristocratic Temper
of Greek Civilization

Introduction

The ancient Greek social spectrum ranged from slaves at one end through a variety of semi-free and free statuses to aristocrats at the other pole. If one turns to modern studies of social conditions it is obvious that slavery receives an extraordinary concentration of attention by both Western and Marxist scholars. The Mainz Akademie, for example, has published a large number of specialized studies on slaves in every conceivable profession and condition; one of the most active students until his recent death was Sir Moses Finley, whose views are summed up in *Ancient Slavery and Modern Ideology*.[1] Aristocrats, on the other hand, are almost completely ignored if not condemned; the most recent level-headed treatment of at least their political place was published in 1896.[2] Elites these days are universally scorned even by academic elites.

This is odd. When one examines ancient literature rather than modern surveys, aristocrats are always in the foreground historically, philosophically, and artistically. They at least had no doubt that they were the most important element in society and established its attitudes and values; slaves on the other hand were only occasionally considered. For the sake of clarity I should offer here a preliminary definition of the term "aristocrats" as being those who shared a cultured pattern of life and values *consciously* conceived and upheld from generation to generation. In all Greek states such groups were limited in numbers but firmly considered themselves the "best"; their claims were normally accepted, even cherished by other, lower classes. If I sometimes use words such as elite, leading elements, upper classes, and so on, this is usually to provide some variation in terminology; if a wider sector is meant I shall try to be specific.

Modern opinion has so exalted the demand for egalitarianism in recent years that the historical existence of social inequality over centuries is muffled or denied; in consequence the aristocrats of ancient Greece too often have been placed in an unwarrantedly hostile light. Here, as in virtually every aspect of their culture, the Greeks were brutally clear-headed in their acceptance of the fact that not all men and women were equal, though one may feel that they at times carried this acceptance to extremes in exploiting their privileged political, economic, and social status. In subsequent chapters, however, we may observe mitigating limitations inherent in the character of Greek political and economic structures.

As between aristocrats and slaves, to return to my opening remarks, I have no doubt that we should devote primary attention to the former as being of decisive importance in the origins and magnificent consolidation of the root of Western civilization; to buttress this perhaps heretical opinion will require a fully rounded assessment of the varied roles of aristocrats in the Hellenic world. In order to reenforce my emphasis on the importance of aristocratic values in Western thought it will be useful at the end to explore briefly, and in general terms the lasting influence of the aristocratic ideal in later European history.

Chapter 1

The Emergence of Aristocrats

In the Homeric world there were heroes but not aristocrats. True, the epic figures were distinguished in birth as Zeus-sprung or the scions of great ancestors; they were frequently given the title of *basileis*, kings; their roles as individual leaders in council and on the battlefield were deliberately emphasized; men and women of this stamp were described as being more delicate and beautiful than ordinary people. The most evident political bond in the Homeric poems was a personal tie between leader and followers, who usually stand as an anonymous mass; when an upstart such as Thersites, ill favored in appearance, sought to speak, he was rudely chastised and silenced.[1]

Even so the Homeric scene contains no aristocrats in the sense in which the term will be used in these pages or as it has been employed in discussions of early modern European society. Both Penelope in the *Odyssey* and Agariste of Sicyon in the early sixth century had eager suitors, who were not dissimilar in their objective. Yet whereas the men who beset Penelope's hall were brawling, uncivilized boors, Agariste's father disdained the unrestrained, drunken dancing of one well-favored youth—a sharp illustration of the great change in cultural attitudes that took place as Hellenic civilization progressed from the epic world in the eighth century into truly historical times.

Not all students of Greek society would accept this distinction, though some have emphasized its existence. A recent survey of Greek ethics points out that in the Homeric age the warriors were preeminent men of wealth and social position, who protected their dependents by their valor in war, and concludes, "This is an aristocratic scale of values."[2] The statements are correct; the inference, however, is premature. For the Homeric world had not yet traveled all the way toward the elaboration of an aristocratic ethos; as has been rightly observed, "Early Greek society was aristocratic in some broad and general sense, yet we have great difficulty in defining the exact sense in which we use that word 'aristocratic'."[3]

By the later eighth century the more advanced areas of Greece were developing in many ways beyond the simple world described in the epics. Geographically the Aegean, formerly isolated from outside influences, burst its bounds and established a vast number of colonies over almost every Mediterranean shore. Economically these new settlements desired products from the homeland, a demand that much accelerated the expansion of local industries and overseas trade even to the Near East. Culturally the potters and other artists as well as writers created far more complicated and advanced modes of expression which in literature could make use of the Greek alphabet borrowed from Semitic origins but improved by the addition of vowels. Politically and socially there was also upheaval that deserves closer inspection; developments that were conjoined at the outset eventually produced uneasy contradictions between the role of the aristocrats and Greek political theory.

The initial political change was the elimination of the Zeus-sprung *basileis*.[4] These kings did not have the financial strengths of medieval and early modern European monarchs; they also lacked firm control over the religious structures of Greek communities; and finally they were not militarily essential to safeguard their local domains in a period when there were no serious external threats or technological development of expensive artillery trains.

The consequence was that they faded away save at Sparta, Argos, and outlying areas in Cyprus. In their place a public official (*prytanis, archon,* etc.) was chosen for one year, often at the outset from one distinguished family; some powers were lodged in the hands of a war leader (*polemarchos*) and a chief priest (*basileus*); to supervise these officials a council (*boule*), again of leading citizens, often served for life or long periods.

Accompanying or immediately following this change the Greek world crystallized out of its earlier tribal organization into a great number of *poleis*, one-celled structures, so to speak, in which all major activity—political, religious, social—was concentrated at one specific point, the *agora*. The inhabitants of each *polis* considered themselves protected by a divinity in whose worship, soon ensconced in a stone temple and altar, they expressed their unity; Sparta, Athens, and other states felt themselves distinct in fundamental values and beliefs from their neighbors.

Since the *polis* emerged during an era in which Greek tribes did not venture except on the sea far from home, it always remained a small district with clear boundaries, often natural in the form of mountains and seas. On the average the Greek states of historic times ranged between 50 and 100 square kilometers, and their population can be estimated at 625 to 1250 by extrapolation from modern rural densities of Aegean islands. Among Greek states can be accounted "large" in terms of citizens only Corinth, Athens, Sparta, Argos, and Thebes on the mainland; Miletus, Samos, and Chios in eastern Greece; Syracuse and a few other western colonies, though these rarely played a significant role in Greek history. That the *poleis* continued to be minuscule reflected the spiritual and religious unity of their inhabitants; as the poet Alcaeus put it, "Not stone or timber make . . . *poleis*; but wheresoever are men who know how to keep themselves safe there are walls and there *poleis*."[5] The *polis* may be described as a "hothouse" in which Greek civilization could develop in many local variations across the seventh and sixth centuries into the polished classical forms of arts and letters. We shall have occasion to revert to the influence of the *polis* in every chapter.

It would be an easy assumption to infer that the nascent aristocracies engineered or seized upon these changes for their own benefit, but the assumption is much too simplicistic. Anthropologists are much interested these days in the development of consciously structured states, and to explain their rise have advanced two very different models. One proposes the emergence of economic and social stratification which led to evolution of a firm structure of political control, the other finds "a response to the need for increased integrative mechanisms in larger and more complex structures."[6] The former model best fits the appearance of early modern monarchies in western Europe and so has been popular from the days of Hobbes, but the latter accords better with the strong sense of communal unity and the poetic evidence surviving from the formative period of Greek civilization; one must always keep in mind the demonstration in Hesiod, as we shall see shortly, that there were nonaristocratic elements of significance in Greek society. The *polis*, in sum, was fundamentally a voluntary union of citizens, bound together tightly by social and religious ties.[7]

Among the officials and councils of these states aristocrats were initially dominant even if their free fellow citizens had latent rights and duties under the rule of law. A brief definition of the aristocratic ethos has already been proferred—and the term "aristocracy" always had as much a moral as a political connotation on Greek thought—but it is high time to be more specific, though indeed all the present work is intended to deepen and intensify our picture of Greek aristocracy. The famous phrase for aristocrats came to be *kaloikagathoi*, as distinguished from the *kakoi* or base; but in the seventh century one cannot be sure that its constituent parts, *kaloi* (beautiful = polished) and *agathoi* (good = preeminent) referred normally to class position rather than individual merit.[8]

In any case such moral or esthetic standards were a later refinement; not until the fifth and following centuries does the term *kaloskagathos* become standard. Essentially an aristocrat was one who was born into an aristocratic family. As Plutarch once commented, "How often in Simonides, Pindar, Alcaeus, Ibycus, and Stesichorus is 'good birth' (*eugeneia*) a matter of praise and honor?" Already in the *Odyssey*, when Menelaus greeted Telemachus and the son of Nestor he observed, "Base churls (*kakoi*) could not beget such sons as you"; one fragment of Archilochus runs, "Enter, because you are well-born (*gennaios*)"; at Athens aristocrats were called Eupatrids, men of "good" fathers.[9] After the *basileis* disappeared in most Greek states there were no hereditary titles, though

Sappho could celebrate her friend Andromeda as "the daughter of kings";[10] but in the seventh and sixth centuries the aristocratic families of any Greek *polis* maintained an essentially closed circle and developed a sure sense that their way of life was morally superior.

Landed wealth, however, was a second important requirement, which is reflected in the term *Gamoroi* at Samos and Syracuse. When Simonides was asked who were *eugeneis*, his reply ran, "Those rich from of old," and seventh-century archons at Athens were chosen "on birth and wealth."[11] How much land did an aristocrat have to have? The simple answer is: enough to maintain his distinct way of life, but in the reforms of Solon at Athens early in the sixth century the leading class, called the *pentekosiomedimnoi*, had annual revenues of 500 *medimnoi* of grain or its equivalent in wine or oil. On the basis of possible maximum crop yields at that time, such a landed revenue would imply possession of over 30 hectares of fair farming land. A simple rural family, on the other hand, could make do in most years with some four hectares. As we shall see in a later chapter, Greek aristocrats were far from wealthy as compared to the great dukes of eighteenth-century England, but even so they were not numerous. Only 300 to 400 Athenian citizens had enough resources to meet the public obligation of maintaining a trireme in the fifth and fourth centuries; Polybius preserves the information that no more than 100 "houses" were considered noble in Locri Epizephyri.[12]

When, then, did men who considered themselves consciously as *kaloikagathoi* emerge in Greek society? Athenian graves suggest that steps toward outward differentiation of the well-to-do can be traced back into the ninth century; the eighth century, however, appears to have been the critical stage in the material evolution of upper-class graves, manifest in provision both of elegant native vases and of foreign luxuries. By the seventh century such tombs were being embellished with marble steles crowned by sphinxes. One of the earliest testimonies to the Greek alphabetic script is an eighth-century jug on which is scratched, "He of all dancers who now dances most gracefully, let him accept this," a suggestion of aristocratic competitiveness.[13] If we had other contemporary written materials from the advanced Greek centers, we might be able to show that the attitudes soon evident in archaic poetry were beginning to be expressed in the later eighth century.

As it is, the next author after Homer whose works have survived is Hesiod of Boeotia, but this poet of the close of the eighth century has never been considered an aristocrat; rather he is usually, but erroneously, labeled a peasant. His is a fascinating, almost unique, voice out of the early Greek world, especially in the poem called *Works and Days*.[14] In its earlier verses Hesiod does show that he did not belong to the uppermost layer of his society, composed of the bribe-swallowing *basileis*, and urges them not to exploit unjustly their strength, like the hawk who seizes the nightingale.

Thereafter, in describing the course of the agricultural year, Hesiod turns to men of his own standing, who are far from being peasants, that is, small farmers dependent on a landlord. Rather he visualizes a well-to-do group capable of finding capital for the purchase of a team of oxen and of female and male slaves and for maritime trips to dispose of surpluses; for himself Hesiod seeks in the heat of summer "a shady rock and wine of Biblis"—imported from Phoenicia at a time when foreign items of any sort were rare and expensive![15] He and his fellows are certainly not aristocrats but are men of some standing; we shall have occasion to return to them in a later chapter, when their leading members can be termed semi-aristocrats, lacking only distinction in birth.

Literary evidence gives firm testimony for the appearance

of the aristocratic outlook a generation or two after Hesiod in the surviving fragments of the poetry of Archilochus of Paros. These show an individual human being, living from day to day, returning hate for hate and love for love. The conscious awareness of aristocratic freedom and liberation from the more superficial bonds of convention are evident in Archilochus; later poets simply made more apparent and extended more widely the line of thought visible in his savage iambics.

Archilochus himself may warn us, however, against overstressing individual self-seeking on the upper-class level and against accepting a common view that group life had been all powerful in early Greece but lost its sway in historic times.[16] The individualism Archilochus voiced had its roots in the magnificent heroes of the *Iliad* and the *Odyssey*, but the sense of social unity that lies below the Homeric surface pervades his verse as well, which was meant to communicate the poet's reflections and to instruct. He was bound more tightly to the fabric of society than a modern individualist could endure.

The first great voice of archaic aristocracy is illuminating in another important aspect. The upper classes of the age had great confidence in their achievements and abilities; at times a heaven-storming audacity, a sense of unfettered experiments, and an almost anarchic outlook are visible. But fear is never far from pride, and as men grew bolder and richer they also became more consciously analytical and never forgot the view expressed in the epic poets and Hesiod that man was a frail creature in an unpredictable world where the gods ruled all. If ill befell, Archilochus exhorted his heart to bear up; "Conqueror, do not overexult; vanished, do not groan prostrate in your house. Savor your successes, mourn your reverses, but not too much. Learn the rhythm which governs the life of men."[17]

Further we need not go at this point in exploring the expression of aristocratic authors down to the days of Plato and Aristotle. Rather, to conclude the survey of the rise of Greek aristocracy, it is time to turn back to a remark just made with respect to Archilochus, to wit, that we must always keep in mind that these leaders, however self-confident, were part of their society. In late medieval France and England there was a good deal of popular criticism and distrust of the incipient aristocracies of that era, expressed, for example, in the outburst of the Jacquerie about 1356 and more continuously in the *ritournelles* composed in France or in the bitter remark of John Ball in 1381,

> Whanne Adam dalfe and Eve span
> Who was thann a gentilman?[18]

This type of evidence does not survive from Greece, but aristocrats were deeply aware of the "pitiless criticism" by their fellow citizens.[19] Religiously, socially, economically, and culturally they were linked by many inherited ties to the rest of society; though they staffed the new executive machinery of state, they had to yield to their compatriots real guarantees of just treatment, which was the fundamental spiritual base of the *polis*. Wherever these guarantees failed seriously in practice, tyrants arose in the course of Greek history, but their role was fleeting; aristocrats, as we shall see in the next chapter, were politically essential, but they were also harnessed within the *polis*.

Chapter 2

Political Power

In many states ruled by monarchs, from the Persian empire on to the France of Louis XIV, aristocrats have had a wide variety of roles. They were the councillors of state and functionaries in ceremonies at the court;[1] they governed satrapies, provinces, and in modern times colonies; in the event of war they were expected to provide leadership and examples of bravery as commanders-in-chief and other officers. Always they were secondary in rank to the rulers, but their honorable positions were often inherited officially or unofficially. In dress and other evidence of high, assured position they were easily distinguished, "les gens de l'épee" in early modern parlance.

In the world of the *polis* matters were very different. The Greek upper classes might dress and otherwise live more elegantly than common folk, but they had neither inherited titles nor positions guaranteed to them by rank. The developed political theory of the *polis*, indeed, denied to its aristocrats any fundamental differentiation. As Aristotle observed repeatedly in his great work, the *Politics*, the objective of the *polis* was to secure justice for its citizens, and consequently equality was a basic necessity. "The members of a political association aim by their very nature at being equal and differing in nothing," or again later, "a state aims at being, as far as it can be, a society composed of equals and peers."[2]

The inherent conflict between this point of view and the natural tendency of aristocrats to claim a special position deserves exploration both on the abstract level and in historical developments. To return to Aristotle, in his heart he preferred aristocracy that "aims at giving pre-eminence to the best," for citizens were after all not equal in goodness; at one point he quotes the contemptuous remark of Antisthenes, "Where are your claws and teeth?" on the assertion of hares that all animals should have equal rights, a comment that may remind one of the query of Stalin, "How many divisions does the Pope have?"[3] But perhaps surprisingly for a student of Plato and a member of the Macedonian court for several years, Aristotle had to admit in his mind that we must consider not only "what is the absolute best, but also what is the best in relation to actual conditions."[4] In this light democracy had practical advantages even if it were not a perfect form of government.

Although we must keep in mind that Aristotle's main intent was political theory and that he viewed its problems mainly from an aristocratic point of view, he did after all live in the *polis* world of the fourth century and had a great fund of knowledge about previous developments. As a great scholar, moreover, he was quite sensitive to the number of variations that attended any phenomenon he was discussing.

A number of factors thus compelled him to the judgment that democracy had to be taken seriously. In the first place, "nowadays, when states have become still larger, we almost say that it is hardly possible for any other form of constitution to exist."[5] Again, of all forms of government feasible in a *polis* democracy was the most moderate and therefore the most stable; "democracy is a form of government which is safer, and less vexed by sedition, than oligarchy."[6] A citizen thus can be defined as "a man who shares in the administration of justice and in the holding of office," and this definition best fits "the citizen of a democracy."[7]

Aristotle, however, judged in his deepest analysis that a mixed constitution, called the *politeia*, was the best form of government, a desirable compromise between the opposed demands of democracy and aristocracy. "In all states there may be distinguished three parts, or classes, of the citizen-body—the very rich, the very poor, and the middle class which forms the mean." The latter is best for listening to reason, but alas in most states *to meson*, the middle element, is small.[8] Here Aristotle links on to a view running back to the general Greek principle, "observe due measure," which is voiced in both the *Odyssey* and Hesiod;[9] by the sixth century it had become more specific in Solon's exhortations to adopt a stance between conflicting factions. Euripides' *Suppliants* presents the same division of citizens into three wings: "The class which is midmost of the three preserves cities, observing such order as the state ordains."[10] The term "class" is, it must be remembered, misleading, for in ancient history there was never a middle class in a modern sense; rather the praise of *to meson* was a view shared by those who disliked faction-alism and civil strife,[11] a very real problem to which Aristotle devoted a good deal of attention in the *Politics*.

Let us turn from theory to the historical development of the Greek world from the eighth century onward. Aristotle provides a scheme that progresses from kingship to aristocracy, the rule of the best, which was perverted into oligarchy. Its excesses in turn produced tyranny, and finally came democracy.[12] The state that most neatly illustrates these changes was Athens, for which we also happen to have the fullest information. As noted in Chapter 1, Athenian aristocrats had supplanted the ancestral kings at least by the early seventh century, and thereafter provided the magistrates and priests of the *polis* under the general supervision of the council of the Areopagus, an aristocratic body recruited from ex-archons and serving for life.

By the first years of the sixth century the struggles of nobles for public office and also their ruthless exploitation of poorer citizens produced an explosion that led to the election in 594—the first reasonably firm date in Greek history—of Solon as archon and reconciler; fortunately the mainsprings of his reforms are visible in the numerous surviving fragments of his poetry. His steps to counter the economic problems of the day were highly successful; his efforts to counter the aggressive behavior of Athenian aristocrats were ingenious but less enduring. He established a council of 400 to serve as steering committee for the citizen assembly which now had a definite place in public life; other provisions permitted anyone to sue on behalf of the wronged and to appeal to popular law courts against improper actions of the magistrates—in Aristotle's eyes this was his most democratic step.

Solon himself was a cautious reformer, and though the *demos* or citizen body thenceforth had to be accounted a conscious element in political processes he himself feared deeply that its participation might be unwise. Repeatedly, he stressed his posture as standing between rich and poor, assuring each its due but no more than that, and in reality he replaced pure aristocracy by a timocracy in which the degree of public activity depended not on ancestry but on wealth, measured in terms of agricultural produce; of the four classes into which he divided the citizen body the lowest, the *thetes*, could exercise only limited influence, especially in the assembly and in the law courts.[13]

Relevant at this juncture are general Aegean developments in the seventh and sixth centuries, particularly as governed by the ever present threat of war. International strife in the *polis* world was always endemic; as Bolkestein observed, "There is one trade, the most extensive which Greek society ever knew, which was naturally carried on by the state, i.e., the waging of war."[14] A widespread change in the organization of Greek armies across the seventh century exerted pressures toward a tighter framework of political life. Early in the period a variety of arms and armor already in existence was assembled to produce the infantry hoplite, with round shield, helmet, breastplate, greaves, and thrusting spear (unlike the javelins of Homeric heroes); and these hoplites were marshalled in a firm infantry mass, the phalanx, several ranks deep. Down to the fourth century this was the formation for battles, which were brutal encounters of similarly equipped citizen warriors.

From Aristotle onward the consequence of the rise of the phalanx has been exaggerated, especially in the hypothetical construct of a politically active "hoplite class,"[15] but there can be no doubt that the new form of military organization required the assembly of all able-bodied men who could provide their own equipment rather than a restricted number of aristocrats who rode to battle horseback. In earlier times, thus, a perhaps legendary law of Cyme gave political rights only to those who owned horses, and the leading class at Chalcis was called the Hippobotai.[16] Now perhaps one-third of the adult male free population could be expected to serve in war. So a wider range of the citizenry had to be motivated to face the dangers of battle; emphasis on patriotism is a common theme in poets of the era, especially Tyrtaeus, but also inevitably participation in political life had to be extended. As in Solon's reforms, the result was generally in the Greek world a movement from pure aristocracy based on birth toward an oligarchy consisting of the well-to-do.

Accelerating this important change was the great economic advance of the Greek world in the seventh and sixth centuries. In minor but still impressive degree the result was the burgeoning of industrial and commercial sectors, which clustered largely about the political centers of the *poleis*. These evolved into true cities in which, as Cyrus the Persian king was later contemptuously to observe, there were "men who have a special meeting place in the center of their city, where they swear this and that and cheat each other."[17] Even though the tale reported by Herodotus may be apocryphal, it casts a vivid light on a significant difference between Near Eastern empires and Greek *poleis*; only Hellas had stationary markets in which enterprising individuals played economic roles.

Greek economic activity also came to be expressed in terms of coinage, which began late in the seventh century and spread like wildfire all over the Aegean and also in overseas colonies; in modern terms this produced a shift from self-sufficient economies to a market-oriented structure, which had varied effects on parts of the *polis* world. In the basic realm of agricultural organization smaller farmers often sank to the level of dependent peasants and in Thessaly, Messenia, and Crete to a status that may loosely be called serfdom or, as it is expressed in ancient terms, "between free and slave"; that is, they were farmers tied to their land and owing regular dues to their lords.

Solon's poetry gives valuable evidence that a powerful

instrument in the similar evolution at Athens was rural debt, which at times even led to the sale abroad as slaves of those who could not meet their obligations. Hesiod noted that a farmer might run into difficulties and have to borrow from a neighbor, but he was expected to do no more than repay the loan without interest when conditions improved. In a money economy oriented toward impersonal markets matters were quite otherwise. Midway in the sixth century the poet Phocylides penned an urgent warning, "Be not the debtor of a *kakos*, or he will annoy you by asking to be paid before his time"—and very probably with interest and harsh penalties for failure to meet the obligation.[18]

How are we to describe these *kakoi*, who became much more evident in the poets of the sixth century? Economically, since they were not of noble stock, they were even less restrained in taking advantage of the opportunities in an era of rapid change. Socially, as we shall see in the next chapter, they sought to live in an aristocratic manner, adopting upper-class values, but scorned by those of ancestral lineage. In modern English terms they might be called the gentry;[19] a more neutral term would be semi-aristocrats. Politically it proved impossible to deny them a considerable place in the state.

The most illuminating discussion of *kakoi* is to be found in the poetry of the sour misanthrope Theognis of Megara, who endured life about 550.[20] Apart from Homer and Hesiod his work is the only corpus down to the fifth century to survive intact—or even more than complete inasmuch as a variety of later work was incorporated into his verse. The genuine poems of Theognis himself were largely addressed to his young boyfriend Cyrnus and had the intention of handing on "the counsels I learned from good men (*agathoi*) in my own childhood. . . . This then I would have thee to know, nor to consort with the *kakoi* but ever to cleave unto the *agathoi*, and at their tables to eat and drink, and with them to sit, and them to please, for their power is great" (19–38).

These views were no different from those of Sappho, Alcaeus, and other earlier poets, but at this point Theognis had to face a very uncomfortable fact: that in reality the *aristoi* were no longer necessarily the wealthiest members of society. The implications of this change, which appears to have been a recent one, run through all the rest of his poetry. The *kakoi* have often gained wealth, and set no end to their search for gain; there is not one boatload of those who put good ahead of money. The result socially is deceit, wiles, lack of trust and gratitude. Since the *kakoi* are at one point described as having once worn goatskins (54–55) they are clearly of rural origins, but they have waxed powerful in the city. In Theognis the term *demos* first begins to have a pejorative meaning as socially inferior.[21]

The only feasible intellectual solution was to assert that the *aristoi* were still best in *arete*, virtue to be gained by inheritance and by conscious effort; men of this stamp shared "qualities of the inner spirit: superior sensibility and sensitivity, wisdom, grace, and ultimately 'moral' goodness."[22] Theognis expressed this argument, but as a man of mediocre nature himself he portrayed aristocratic life largely in terms of dinners, noble music, and drinking in pleasant conversation. He was an indoorsman, uninterested in hunting or "evil war," though he granted that one must fight for one's *polis*.

Such a solution did not resolve all the troubles Theognis faced, for he had also to admit that nonaristocratic elements "corrupt the common folk" and reach political office. It was they, in his view, who caused trouble in the state as a consequence, which could lead to internal discord and even to tyranny. Clearly by the later sixth century the *kakoi* had gained significant weight in many Greek states.

After examining general developments in the seventh and sixth centuries it is time to return to Athens, for its evolution was to follow a very different path from most of its neighbor *poleis*. Here an unusual solution to the problem of fitting an aristocracy into the fundamental egalitarian theory of the *polis* was to be perfected, though only after a detour into tyranny.

The roots of this diversion were local. Solon's efforts to check aristocratic divisiveness were so unsuccessful that the state fell at times into chaos. So the way lay open for a cunning, determined man to seize power as a tyrant. The first two efforts by Pisistratus were thwarted by his fellow aristocrats, but in 546 he came back from exile with a force of mercenaries. Internally he was favored also by elements in the villages and burgeoning city, who might if we had more evidence be called representatives of the *kakoi*. He was this time successful in gaining and keeping power until his death in 527. To appease his fellow nobles he allowed them to continue to hold offices of state and paraded constitutional behavior, but he also aided the common folk by improving the water supply of Athens and regularizing its *agora*; farmers were assisted by loans even if they also had to pay taxes, an unusual requirement in ancient Greece.

His sons Hippias and Hipparchus peacefully succeeded him, but in 514 Hipparchus fell victim to a plot led by two aristocratic homosexuals, Harmodius and Aristogeiton, who were celebrated in later years as "tyrant slayers" in drinking songs at aristocratic symposia. Hippias naturally became more despotic; in 510 the Alcmeonid family, which had been in voluntary exile, secured the aid of Sparta, the most powerful state in Greece and in principle opposed to tyranny, to oust him.

Once again the Athenians could engage in factional politics. The conservative aristocrat Isagoras was elected archon in 508 and sought to put back the clock, especially by purging the citizen rolls of aliens who had crept in during the years of the tyrants. His opponent, Cleisthenes of Alcmenid stock, was weaker in upper-class support; by way of counterbalance he "called to his aid the common people" with the battlecry of *isonomia* or equal rights.[23] In the next few years Cleisthenes totally recast the structure of Athenian government so that authority lay firmly in the hands of the citizen assembly, guided by a yearly changing council of 500 that was chosen by an elaborate system of voting districts so that no one area or class could dominate it. With only a few minor alterations Cleisthenes' reforms endured well over 200 years, the longest-lived and most complete democracy the Western world has yet seen as measured by the ultimate power of those allowed to sit on the rocky hillside of the Pnyx.

Twice, to be sure, the Athenians had to yield the power of their assembly, in 411 and again in 404 as a result of the disasters of the Peloponnesian war, but each time the break was brief. Ironically enough, Cleisthenes was almost forgotten whereas Solon's ideal conception of the *polis* made him a lasting figure of reverence. Perhaps Cleisthenes' actions smacked too much of opportunism, yet more than once in history opportunists have had greater effects than they planned in seeking their own advantage.

Across the great years of the fifth century, when arts and letters flourished at home and Athens built up a sea-based empire, it entrusted its democracy to military and political leaders of aristocratic origins—Themistocles, Aristides, Cimon, Pericles—but the citizenry kept them on a short leash; all but Pericles were sent into exile, and even Pericles was once briefly removed from office. In the dismal years of the struggle against Sparta, 431–404, some figures including Nicias and Alcibiades continued to be aristocrats, but others such as Cleon and Cleophon were of more modest origins.

By the fourth century a clear division between political and military leaders had evolved. Those who spoke in the assembly and guided its decisions remained often of upper-class backgrounds whereas generals were often men who rose on performance. Demosthenes' ancestry cannot certainly be traced earlier than his grandfather; the noted financial and religious reformer Lycurgus, on the other hand, was a member of one of the oldest and most prestigious Attic families.[25] When the Athenians sent an embassy to the Persians, which Alexander unfortunately captured, its members were Iphicrates, son of the great general; Dropeides, of a family going back to the days of Solon; and Aristogeiton, who may have been descended from the tyrant-slayer. None were prominent politicians; they had presumably been chosen for their status, though Darius might not have recognized this honor.[26]

Beneath the surface there still lay in fourth-century Athens a conflict between elitist insistence that the well-born should rule and the fundamental principles of democracy, as has recently been explored in a magnificent study, but the resulting tensions were admirably kept in check by subtle, unwritten compromises.[27]

Most Greek states, however, continued to be governed by oligarchies of their well-to-do citizens that had at least a tincture of aristocratic insistence on the ancestral rights of good breeding.[28] The Spartan community is often taken as the oligarchic foil to democratic Athens, but we cannot peer deeply enough into its deliberate obscurities to determine precisely how its complex structure of assembly, council of elders, ephors, kings, *perioikoi* (second-class citizens), and helots interacted. As far as one can judge, it was as unusual in its own way as was Athens. Corinth, Thebes, and other oligarchic states are more visible though they display a bewildering variety of patterns of political organization; as in the federal system of the United States today one of the enduring strengths and sources of innovation, politically as well as culturally, lay in the local diversity of the *polis* world.

By the fifth and fourth centuries even oligarchic states had an assembly of citizens, though at times the right of attendance was limited by property requirements and other checks. Usually the assembly could only express approval or dissent, especially for treaties; it was not as independent as it was at Athens. Rather, important decisions were commonly in the hands of a council limited in numbers and chosen from senior citizens for life or otherwise clearly reflecting the power of the upper classes. The officials who carried out the decrees were also normally chosen by vote rather than by lot from the wealthy and aristocratic level but everywhere only for one year; oligarchs trusted each other as little as did democrats.[29]

Why should this pattern of government obtain so widely? One simple answer is that the average free citizen, even at Athens, had to work either in the fields or in potteries, smithies, and other industrial establishments to earn his livelihood and could spare neither time nor energy to consider public problems. Furthermore, most men were not educated sufficiently to promote self-confidence in their own judgment and hearkened more easily to the counsels of those who had the blessings of leisure. Above all, as we shall see in succeeding chapters, the upper classes of the *poleis* were dominant socially, economically, culturally, and religiously; it was almost inevitable that this superiority extended to the political realm.

Still, one must always keep in mind the spiritual principle on which the *polis* rested; as Aristotle put it, "a state aims at being, as far as it can be, a society composed of equals and peers." In actual life the rich, leisured classes and the working poor were deeply sundered, and at times the division could bring upheaval and even civil war (*stasis*), illuminated especially in the pages of Thucydides on the outburst at

Corcyra at the beginning of the Peloponnesian war, but visible far too often on other occasions.

"In the awful war of factions, in which Greek states were at all times engaged, the historians have no hesitation in putting the blame on the oligarchs," observed Whibley in his concluding remarks, but this is somewhat too pessimistic a view.[30] Civil strife was spasmodic, exceptional, rather than the rule; otherwise Greek political structures would have shattered. Aristotle's advice that in democracies the rich should not be exploited ruthlessly whereas in oligarchies the well-to-do should not abuse their power was not always observed in practice,[31] but the basic thrust of the theory of the *polis*, inherited from a simple age of communal unity, always had its influence as a check and force for balance. On the surface, however, Greek history was the product, save to some degree at Athens, of the upper classes; even more certainly its accounts were written by and for those classes.

Chapter 3

Social Position

The social role of the aristocratic class, as a pinnacle over commoners, resident aliens (especially at Athens), and slaves, was consolidated in the formative era of Greek civilization. True aristocrats were very limited in numbers in a world that could support only a very restricted upper class. So too in modern times the leading elements can be counted at most as 1½% of the population in France and other areas during the Old Regime.[1] But aristocrats knew who they were—they were the men (and women) who had ancestors. At Athens the reformer Cleisthenes tried to reduce the significance of this factor by a rule that Themistocles, son of Neocles, for example, should be registered on citizen rolls simply as

Themistocles of the tribe Phrearrhi, but patronymics continued to be used widely in society.

The place of aristocrats was not only well defined in
practice; it was also unchallenged. In the preceding chapter
we observed the rise of the *kakoi*, nonaristocrats who economically and politically in their patterns of life aped their
betters as much as they could. Plato has Socrates complain
in the *Protagoras* about "the wine parties of second-rate and
commonplace people" who have to have a female flute-player
"being too uneducated to entertain themselves."[2] There was,
after all, no alternative system of values and modes of relax-
ation; those changes in early modern Europe that produced
a true bourgeoisie with its own life style in dress, housing,
and other visible marks could not have occurred in the *polis*
world, limited as its commercial and financial sectors were.[3]

Discussing the parade of modern luxury, the noted
French historian Braudel observes, "The privileged and the
onlookers—the masses who watch them—must of course
agree to a certain amount of connivance,"[4] but the term
"connivance" implies too conscious an attitude among the
ordinary Greek citizens in accepting without serious objection
the social pre-eminence of aristocrats. There were no French
or Russian revolutions to challenge their position even though
they might occasionally abuse it politically; in counterbalance
there are "few signs of aristocratic prejudice in the poetry of
the seventh and sixth centuries B.C."[5]

The aristocratic way of life and the models it provided
became ever more consciously structured as the Greek world
evolved into the classical period and were firmly set against
an urban background in the more advanced communities,
particularly but not exclusively at Athens, even though this
state also perfected a democratic political system. Aristocrats
commonly lived in the cities or at least had townhouses as
well as rural abodes.[6] Aristocratic ways came to be urban

ways; Sappho contemptuously dismissed some poor wench as a "farm girl in farm-girl finery . . . even ignorant of the way to lift her gown over her ankles."[7]

The vehicles for aristocratic expression and its maintenance were many, though at least in one case we must be cautious in accepting a widespread modern view. Every discussion of Greek society contains a picture of the clan or *genos* as a powerful grouping of families especially on the upper-class level. Belief in the presence of this institution in Greek life owes much to the models provided by Roman *gentes* (it is always dangerous, though, to transfer concepts from Rome to Greece), Scotch clans, and anthropological parallels. In truth, however, the *genos* must simply be discarded as a figment of learned imagination down at least into the fifth century. A lengthy, well-buttressed dissertation by a French scholar has demolished it as a modern fabrication and has shown that the only true *gene* were the royal clans of Sparta and some priestly clans here and there, as at Eleusis.[8]

The fundamental unit of Greek social organization on all levels was rather the *oikos* or family, which included the land and other possessions necessary for its survival; a colony, for example, may properly be described as "an organic group of *oikoi*."[9] Above or around the *oikos* were territorial units ranging from village to *ethnos* and later the *polis*, religious groupings about local shrines, brotherhoods or phratries, ties between aristocrats and followers, and many others. Greeks of any class, male or female, adult or child, were thus linked to their comrades by many ties of different sorts, which they usually accepted both in their limitations and in their support of the uncertainties of life.

Primarily among aristocrats kinship did have a very important role in exacting blood-money or vengeance for a murder, a theme that infuses Aeschylus' great trilogy, the *Oresteia*, and its influence in determining who married whom was significant, though not prescriptive as often in primitive tribes of Polynesia and Africa. Hesiod's advice in marriage seems to be totally oblivious of kinship; "a man should marry a maiden who is much younger . . . for a man has nothing better than a good wife and, again, nothing worse than a bad one who roasts her man without fire."[10] Hesiod, indeed, does not reflect aristocratic attitudes and on this plane marriages and companion dowries were often very carefully regulated as we can detect in the family trees of leading Athenian figures.[11] It must be noted, however, that the purpose of such links was essentially social, unlike the political use of marriage among Roman aristocrats of the Late Republic.

The upper classes of the Greek world again differed from their Roman successors, but were more similar to aristocrats in modern Europe, in their tendency to form international marriages. The suitors of Agariste, daughter of the tyrant of Sicyon, hailed from an amazing number of other states, identified carefully in a passage in Herodotus; at Athens Themistocles, Cimon, and others had foreign wives, and Pericles' only surviving son was born to his mistress Aspasia of Miletus. Inasmuch as Pericles had been instrumental in passing a law in 450 that citizens had to be of citizen stock on both sides, this caused him trouble mitigated only by the passage of a special decree.

More generally, foreign marriage could always leave its descendants open to the charge of being "of bad parentage," but the potential advantages were many, especially when joined to inherited ties of guest-friendship (as in the Homeric tale of Diomedes and Glaucus).[12] Aristocrats never knew when they might be forced into exile, as were Sappho and many others down through the time of Herodotus, or otherwise need friends in other states. A fragment of Solon significantly describes a happy man as one who has "dear children, wholehooved steeds, hunting hounds, and a friend in foreign parts."[13] These ties were reenforced by the assembly of athletes in the great games or festivals at the shrines of Olympia, Delphi, and elsewhere that became popular in the seventh and sixth centuries. The consolidation of a widely shared Hellenic concept of aristocratic values and virtues owed much to these international connections.

Abroad and at home aristocrats were marked by a characteristic their Homeric forebears had lacked. In peacetime Odysseus plowed; Penelope wove. Later Penelopes continued to weave and to spin, but their husbands, the descendants of Odysseus, no longer worked on the land. "Leisure," Aristotle pronounced, "is a necessity, both for growth in goodness and for the pursuit of political activities."[14]

Aristocrats lived without physically laboring as did their lower-class fellow-citizens, but they were not thereby necessarily idle. The duties of a *polis*, as Aristotle suggests, might take a great deal of a man's time, talking in the *agora* with his fellows about civic matters (and gossiping, too), attending assemblies or councils, serving from time to time as an unpaid magistrate of state. *Arete* (excellence) required doing one's duty courageously in battle. One mark of the happiest man Solon had ever known, Tellus of Athens, was his glorious death in a battle between Athenians and Megarians where he secured the victory: "The Athenians gave him a public funeral on the spot where he fell, and paid him the highest honors."[15]

There were private, as well as public activities, though almost always in groups. Greek life was communal and did not encourage rugged individualism save in the ostentation of tyrants; as noted earlier even Archilochus, who first expressed a strongly personal outlook, was bound by the norms of his society. Communal meals, *syssitia*, had been well known in early Greece but then died out except at Sparta and a few other conservative areas. Drinking parties, *symposia*, on the other hand remained enduringly popular everywhere; these demand careful inspection as a strong bond for aristocratic unity. They took place in the late afternoon and early evening in the men's room (*andron*) in the houses of the well-to-do and had a formal character under a master of the revels, who decided how much wine to add to the water—the less the more likely was a drunken party—and also pronounced the theme for mutual entertainment. Guests, reclining on couches beside the tables, were expected to be able to sing a song, perhaps at Athens in praise of the tyrant-slayers, tell an amusing or unusual story, or in Plato's milieu debate the nature of truth or beauty.

In the quotation given earlier from his *Protagoras*, on the efforts of the *kakoi* to imitate their betters at symposia, Plato goes on to assert that "where the drinkers are *kaloikagathoi* you will find no girls piping or dancing or harping." This perhaps is somewhat too noble a picture; the giver of a symposium might well stroll earlier in the day to the *agora*, both at Athens and in other cities, to engage the services of a skilled female *aulos*-player to accompany his guests' songs.[16] The host Callias in Xenophon's *Symposium* went so far as to contract with a Syracusan impresario to provide an *aulos*-player, a girl acrobat who somersaulted in and out of a circle of sword blades, a boy lyre-player and a dancer.[17] Young ladies of dubious character, scantily clad if at all, appear in vase-paintings to relieve the sexual tensions of the participants, especially by fellatio, or even to hold the head of one who had to regurgitate after too much wine.[18] Their elders, true, might engage in more restrained activities such as debating public issues; very probably many problems were quietly settled in aristocratic symposia.[19]

Symposia, however, were limited in occurrence. The bulk of an aristocrat's day was free for other pursuits, which tended to be of an athletic or out-of-doors nature; no man of standing remained in his house with his womenfolk all the time. An aristocrat's *arete* could be displayed in many ways, such as hunting on foot with one's lean hounds. The prey was no longer the wild boar of Meleager's hunt; if lions ever had existed in Greece they had retreated to the fastnesses of Macedonia. Today on Sunday one often sees Athenians pour out to the countryside to hunt, sometimes on motorcycles, shotguns strapped to their backs, and blaze away at anything that moves, even a tiny bird; in antiquity an Athenian cup shows a perhaps usual trophy, a brace of rabbits.[20]

Athletics proper became an ever more regular part of upper-class life, a position it has held to the present day in European successors. In the local gymnasia aristocrats vied in running and other individual competition; team sports were virtually unknown and the proper objective was to show good form, not simply to win. Those who had special abilities could enter the international contests, and success here brought great renown.[21] One victor from Sybaris in the mid-sixth century erected a small shrine to Athena with only a tithe of the rewards he had received for his Olympic victory.[22]

Physically able nonaristocrats might also win athletic prominence, but they could not hope to engage in one very significant range of upper-class competition. Raising horses "is the task of the most well-to-do,"[23] for only they could afford to own horses and chariots, a prime example of what Thorstein Veblen labeled "conspicuous consumption," inasmuch as horses were difficult to maintain in the meadowless Greek landscape, and were of no economic utility. But horses and chariots appear abundantly from eighth-century figurines and vases (especially at Argos) onward. Names compounded with Hippo- were common on the upper-class level; the young wastrel Pheidippides ("thrifty in regard to horses") in Aristophanes' *Clouds*, likely rather to bankrupt his father with stable fees, chariots, and dream of victory in the races, was the product of centuries of horse-loving aristocrats.

In all these aristocratic activities masculine dominance was obvious and unquestioned. The ultimate test of membership in the upper classes was derivation from a "well-born" family, and in ancient physiological thought the seed of the father was the root of the offspring. Women were indeed necessary as mothers, but from the curses of Agamemnon on the female sex was not often highly praised; the most vitriolic attack is that by Semonides of Amorgos, who likened females to sows, vixen, bitches, and others, and only in one type, that of the bee, could find anything good to say.[24]

The physical attributes of male sexuality were portrayed by the arts—on coins, on vases, in wayside pillars of Hermes—without the scruples that have marked most centuries of modern Western civilization. Homosexuality does not openly appear in the epics, but at least by the sixth century it was accepted on aristocratic levels. At Sparta, Thebes, and elsewhere conjunction of male lovers was even made a part of military organization; at Athens favored youngsters were much sought after and were hailed on vases as *kalos* or "beautiful." To be young and have friends was the acme of masculine desire—and the counterpart, old age, was the worst of ills.[25]

Always, to be sure, the words of masculine writers must be taken with some reserve while appraising the relations of the sexes; in the female voice of the period, that of Sappho, there is not one word of bitterness on the subject. At Athens from the ninth century on rich graves were almost entirely of females, and the tombstone reliefs of classical times abundantly reveal grief at the loss of a beloved wife. Politically and legally women were dependent and had no part in many aspects of social intercourse, but they did not live in a harem atmosphere, and their beauty, no less than that of men, was appreciated.[26] Elpinice, the sister of Cimon, was quite capable of openly interceding for her brother in exile and securing from Pericles his return to Athens.

If an aristocratic pattern is to be vigorous, it must be transmitted from generation to generation. The sons of Roman senators could attend sessions of the Senate and hear Cicero and others spin golden webs of Latin oratory; in the great hall of a Roman mansion hung waxen masks, *imagines*, of famous ancestors. These were taken down on the occasion of a funeral and worn in the procession; in the Forum an orator stepped forward to recite the deeds of the relevant forebear. These formal remembrances of ancestral dignity were not open to Greek aristocrats, but from the Dipylon vases at Athens in the eighth century, which depict stately escorts of fellow warriors, on to classical times aristocrats were buried with pomp. Their graves were often crowned by male and female statues of youths, the *kouroi* and *korai*,[27] and at least in family tradition memories of great predecessors remained green.

The most useful mode of passing on aristocratic virtues was conscious guidance into proper paths by emphasis on ancestors and also life within the family, but as time progressed formal schools were established.[28] Among aristocratic schools the most famous was that conducted by Sappho for maidens from many parts of Asia Minor, but other instructors taught music and similar skills on a level above that of primary education; later we shall have occasion to return to the role of professional teachers of rhetoric and logic, the sophists, at Athens.

In modern societies, however, despite the extensive dedication of interest and revenues to educational systems, peer pressure remains an important factor in establishing real patterns of values and behavior. Ancient Greek nobles were even more ruthlessly subject to conscious scrutiny by their equals and also by their inferiors in the *agora*; an aristocrat must exemplify the virtues of his class. Glory and repute were gained from the judgment of one's fellow men, which was expressed in such adjectives as *agathos* or such nouns as *time* (public repute) and *kleos* (fame). In bitter verse Theognis urged his young friend Cyrnus "ever to cleave unto the *agathoi*."

Almost instinctively men of the upper classes were distinguishable by their behavior toward each other and toward their inferiors, and very possibly as well by their mode of speech. Equally evident were physical marks of luxury. *Habrosyne*, or luxury, is a leitmotif of the poetry of the seventh and sixth centuries; *tryphe* (daintiness) is a contemptuous word that was used later for the most part. The concept, to be sure, is always a relative matter; an Assyrian monarch would have scorned a Greek house as a hovel, and one may doubt that Greek painted pottery would have developed as far as it did if its purchasers had been able to afford to load their shelves with gold and silver vessels. Still, the upper classes of Greece seized all available opportunities for a more elegant life.

Alcinous in the *Odyssey* boasts that "feasting, stringed instruments and dancing, changes of clothing, warm baths, and the pleasures of love are ever dear to us." By the sixth century the picture had become more precise in Xenophanes' condemnation of the Colophonians, who "learned useless luxuries of the Lydians while they were free of hateful despotism, and went into the marketplace clad in all-purple robes, went not less than a thousand in all, proudly rejoicing in gold-adorned hair and bedewing their odor with studied anointings." Much the same portrait is drawn by the poet Asius of the Samians, "swathed in beautiful vestments, with snowy tunics that swept the floor of wide earth; and golden headpieces surmounted them, like cicadas; their tresses waved in the breeze and their golden bands and bracelets wrought with carving circled their arms."[29] Greek aristocrats nonetheless were not as officially distinguished in dress as Roman aristocrats with their purple-edged togas or early modern nobles with puffed trunks and rapiers of honor; Thucydides notes in passing that the Athenians were "the first to lay aside arms and only recently gave up binding their hair with golden cicadas . . . the simple dress which is now common was first worn at Sparta."[30]

Even in food there could be distinction. Alcman boasted that he ate "not what is nicely prepared but demands common things like the rabble"; the Sybarites, who became a symbol of luxury, were said to have given patents to cooks who devised new dishes; by the sixth century Hipponax could label barley as "fodder for slaves."[31] Better diets and exemption from grueling physical labor permitted the upper classes to live longer than did the rest of the populace, dead as a rule in their 30s, though the results of overindulgence in symposia may have to some degree countered these favorable factors.[32]

For other outward aspects of life we have less secure testimony. The aristocratic dead, as noted earlier, were buried more magnificently than others. Though house patterns are almost unknown, interesting recent evidence has begun to reveal that in classic times the well-to-do of Athens may have lived in large mansions; vase paintings and other evidence attest the presence of well-turned furniture and tableware.[33]

Eventually the attitudes, way of life, and values of aristocrats were consolidated in the overarching fourth-century concept of *paideia* (culture). It is, however, dangerous to read back too much from the pages of Isocrates, Plato, and Aristotle to earlier centuries, though the ethical treatises of Aristotle in particular are useful checkpoints and have often been quoted in preceding pages. Also troublesome is the tendency to take *paideia* as a purely aristocratic outlook. Fundamentally the Greek upper classes shared the values and ethical standards of Hellenic civilization as a whole, though they voiced and exemplified those views in a more conscious manner. So too it has been observed for the Russian gentry of the nineteenth century that "their faith, their tastes, their essential fears and hopes were the same (although they little suspected it) as those of the common people whose ignorance they sneered at."[34] Even so the social concept of *paideia* in its developed form was to be passed on to Rome and thence to modern Europe as a standard for upper-class behavior, one of the greatest legacies from ancient Greece which even today has not lost its power in many areas and circles—why otherwise should there have to be continuing outbursts of anger at "elites"?

Chapter 4

Economic Power

The economic strength of the Greek upper classes rested on
one simple fact: they controlled the land. All across ancient
history the well-to-do were masters in their states or cities
and as has been observed for the Roman Empire they were
"more likely to derive their wealth from the ownership of
land than from active participation in manufacture or even
commerce."[1] This emphasis on rural property remained true
well into the nineteenth century after Christ; not until the
closing decades of that century and still more in our own age
have economists come to judge that industrial, commercial,
and financial sectors are the most important into which to
deploy capital and to seek the profits therefrom.

While it is not likely that Greek agriculture often produced more than limited dividends, those who were masters
of the rural landscape gained an even greater advantage—
they also controlled almost all the population of a *polis* either
directly or indirectly.[2] Accordingly, aristocrats tended to hold
on to their land. It has often been argued that an ancestral
plot (*kleros*) could not be alienated outside the family before
the fifth century, but a variety of evidence proves otherwise.
Hesiod's father migrated from Asia Minor to Boeotia, where
he acquired a farm; the poet himself advised his auditors to
honor the gods "so you may buy another's holding (*kleros*)
and not another yours." Aristotle's assertion that "to part
with family estate was one of the things that were 'not
done,' " does not prove the inference that it could not be
done.[3] Normally, nonetheless, formal sale or transfer of land
rights was unlikely in so rurally based a world; political
citizenship and economic security rested on an independent
connection to land.[4]

Various areas saw their smaller farmers of earlier times
reduced to the level of bondsmen or serfs, though true agricultural slavery was uncommon in the Greek world.[5] Usually rural domains were not large in view of the fragmented
geographical nature of Greek landscapes; the largest known
at Athens, as noted earlier, ran only about 50 hectares, though
"in fifth- and fourth-century Athens there were landowners
possessing from three to six estates in different part of At-
tica."[6] Those who could be expected to serve as hoplites
probably were masters of at least 12 hectares; free farmers
after the Solonian reforms would scarcely have been able to
cope with more than 4 hectares unless they drew in outside
labor at critical points in the agricultural cycle.[7]

How were the larger holdings managed? In modern
times nobles relied on stewards, factors, and the like to bear
day-to-day responsibilities; this was probably the case also in

ancient Greece, though our evidence is very limited. Cimon's liberality to his fellow demesmen was famous, but he was absent from Athens so often on military operations that he must have had a resident aide. For Pericles we do have the comment in Plutarch's life that he arranged his paternal estate so "that it might neither through negligence be wasted or lessened, nor yet, being so full of [public] business as he was, cost him any great trouble or time with taking care of it." Thus he sold "all his yearly products and profits" in a lump and bought on the market for his household needs—obol-pinching and keeping precise records to the discontent of his family. "His manager in all this was a single servant, Evangelos by name."[8] To secure fuller information on the careful management of agricultural resources for economic gain we must come down to Hellenistic Egypt where the financial director for Ptolemy II had an extremely astute manager, Zenon, many of whose detailed records have survived on papyri.[9]

The picture usually drawn of upper-class concentration on landed possessions may as a whole stand, but before we accept it as representing the exclusive interest of the well-to-do further reflection is necessary on the nonagricultural aspects of the economy. For example, Demosthenes, on reaching his majority, brought suit against his guardians for the recovery of his inheritance. The estate he itemized to the jury under two headings is rather surprising: "(1) the active (*energa*), which included 32 or 33 slave swordmakers, bringing in 3000 drachmas a year; another 20 slaves engaged in the manufacture of furniture, 1200 drachmas annually; and 8000 drachmas on loan at 12%; (2) the inactive: raw materials on hand at his father's death nine years before, worth 15,000 drachmas, the house worth 3000, the furniture and his mother's jewelry, 8000 in cash in a strong-box at home, a maritime loan of 7000 drachmas, and 4700 on deposit in two banks

and with a relation."[10] Land proper does not appear at all;
Demosthenes was rather, in Bolkestein's summary, "accus-
tomed to make [his fortune] bear interest in many ways" as
a capital-investor, living on the interest of his money.[11]

Demosthenes' family was not, indeed, of aristocratic
stock,[12] so it may have been willing to extend the employment
of its capital more widely in the thriving Athenian industry
and trade of the fifth and fourth centuries. How far did the
aristocrats do the same, or alternatively shun this area?

Industry may be dismissed briefly. Men of standing were
not likely to sully their fingers or break their backs in the
physical toil of stonemasons, smiths, potters, and other
trades. Even so they did have an important, twofold role:
they were the consumers who bought the wares of craftsmen,
and they provided to a large degree the capital necessary for
the purchase of the slaves who furnished a valuable share of
the labor. The swordmakers and furniture fabricators of Demosthenes have already been noted; even more remarkable
was the fact that Nicias, of aristocratic stock, owned a thousand slaves, whom he leased out to the entrepreneurs running
the state silver mines of Laurium.

Commerce was another matter. Retail trade, such as
that in ribbons, could be left to vendors, many of them
women, but large-scale activity especially by sea required
wider attention. One principal mark of the Aegean world in
and after the eighth century was overseas voyaging, and this
was without doubt initially in the hands of aristocrats.

Sappho's brother Charaxus, for example, carried wine
to Egypt and there fell in love with a courtesan, to Sappho's
disgust; Solon also engaged in foreign commerce in order to
recoup his father's prodigality.[13] Colaeus of Samos, blown off
course to Egypt as far as Tartessus whence he gained so much
that he had to replace his stone anchors by silver ingots, and
the later Sostratus of Aegina, who dedicated a statue in the

Greek shrine of Etruscan Pyrgi, very probably were both men of the leading classes inasmuch as they entered Herodotus' pages.[14]

It was, after all, aristocrats who had surplus resources that could be ventured abroad and also were leaders, able to face possible hostile resistance on foreign shores. Contrary to the views of many modern scholars, moreover, both they and the potters described in Hesiod's *Works and Days* sought earnestly after wealth. Already in the epics Odysseus was taunted as not looking like an athlete, that is, a man of leisure, but "one, who faring to and fro with his benched ship, is a captain of sailors who are merchantmen, one who is mindful of his freight, and has charge of a home-borne cargo, and the gains of his greed."[15] Solon categorized the diverse ways of gaining wealth and concluded that those who are richest "have twice the eagerness that others have"; his contemporary Alcaeus quoted Aristodemus—a Spartan no less—as saying that "wealth makes the man."[16] At first aristocratic seafaring might not have been much distinguished from piracy and coastal raids, but eventually it settled into more ordered communications.[17]

Aristocrats were also the men most interested in the wares that could be acquired in the advanced workshops of the Near East—ivory, glass, faience, perfumes, ointments, and spices (many of which had names of Semitic root)—for such luxuries were the backbone of the earliest overseas trade.[18] Greek lands, even including Athens down to the time of Solon, fed themselves, though they did have need for foreign slaves, metals, wool, stone, and other bulk items.[19] Hesiod drank wine of Biblis while relaxing in the heat of summer, and to a remarkable degree men and also women of the upper classes desired wools dyed in Tyrian purple and fine linen. Since textiles do not survive well in archeological contexts this item is often overlooked, but even in modern times the textile trade has been very significant; in the English colonies of North America in the eighteenth century the main import consisted of English, Irish, and German cloth and textiles.[20]

By the later sixth century aristocrats had become more conscious of the duties and limitations of their position and largely yielded long-distance trade to professional shippers, but as they withdrew into the background their interest in this realm did not disappear. The men who scurried about the Aegean and farther afield had to have capital to outfit their ships and finance cargoes. To an extent that we cannot measure they may have done so out of their own resources, but at least occasionally they had to secure a bottomry loan at rates up to 33.33%—Demosthenes' estate, it may be remembered, included such a loan, and in one of his orations a money-lender/banker asserted that without the support of men of his type "no ship, shipper, or sailor can put to sea."[21] And who provided the money to the banker? Undoubtedly the well-to-do of Athens; in imperial Rome as in early modern times the rich supplied funds by the back door to large-scale traders.[22] Nor did aristocrats totally surrender the field; Andocides, who traced his ancestry back to Hermes via Odysseus and Telemachus, actually engaged in maritime commerce throughout the winter in the late fifth century and after his return from exile "continued to think and act like the businessman he had turned himself into."[23] It is unsafe to assume that the word *kerdos* (profit) totally disappeared from aristocratic lips even after the developed ethos of the class frowned on undue interest in economic activities. Aristotle in his *Nicomachean Ethics* judiciously stressed the need for a competence but not a search for gain per se.[24]

Through control of the land and the revenues from investments the well-to-do economically commanded the Greek communities, sometimes almost completely, though at Ath-

ens only in major degree, and used every available opportunity
to enjoy an elegant, luxurious life. Modern hostility toward
elites swiftly rises into view at this point in the common
assertion that aristocrats in all ages simply spend money rather
than improving the economic machinery of their world in a
bourgeois fashion. Thus early modern aristocracies were re-
proved as being engaged in "the unjust, unhealthy, brilliant
and anti-economic utilisation of any surplus produced in a
given society."[25] An interesting study of men who partici-
pated especially in the Thirty Years' War of the seventeenth
century after Christ suggests that their wealth was committed
to building mansions and to acquiring adornments such as
gold necklaces.[26] Only one noted scholar, to my knowledge,
finds merit in this type of expenditure. Writing about early
modern English aristocrats, G. M. Trevelyan raises the ques-
tion as to how else the English nobles could have expended
their money save by building magnificent houses in a period
when stocks, bonds and general loans were unknown and land
was not easily bought—but then Trevelyan is nowadays generally dismissed as an elitist.[27]

If a phenomenon recurs frequently in different historical
societies, then there must be significant reasons for its presence; and an understanding of those reasons will be more
useful than the common expression of indignation or reproof.
Braudel, just quoted, also observes that luxury "scarcely
changes at all" as a concept accepted both by privileged and
unprivileged classes and, as he notes, both Mauss and Sombart
emphasized the role of luxury in promoting demands on
artists and others in early modern Europe. So too the aristocrats of ancient Greece stimulated the amazing outburst of
Hellenic civilization by their patronage of the arts and crafts,
as we shall see in the next chapter.

Some modern aristocracies unfortunately have been
largely parasitical and have been overthrown in violent rev-

olutions. In Greece the political, social, and economic position of the upper classes was too deeply anchored ever to
be seriously threatened; even the Athenian democracy commonly entrusted its leadership to men sprung from aristocratic families of high standing. The upper classes of Athens,
however, paid a heavy price both personally and economically.
If they were wealthy enough to afford hoplite armor or horses,
they had to be prepared to face the dangers inherent in the
almost unceasing wars of the fifth and fourth centuries; an
inscription of 460 or 459 lists no less than 177 men of one
Athenian tribe who died in one year in Cyprus, Egypt, and
elsewhere, including two generals (an Athenian tribe might
have had in the order of 4000 adult male citizens, but the
number who in practice might be drafted is much reduced
if one takes into account the men of age and those mentally
and physically incompetent).[28] The well-to-do also had to
bear liturgies, that is, the obligation to put on plays and
choruses at the Dionysiac festival, to assume the responsibility
for a trireme for a year, and to meet other unpaid chores of
state that could be very expensive. One trierarch thus reveals
his expenditures in recruiting rowers, providing better tackle,
and even paying the men for their food when the general
failed to do so.[29]

Charity was not yet a virtue in ancient thought; one of
the duties of the city commissioners at Athens was to supervise a band of public slaves who removed the bodies of
those unfortunates who died on the streets overnight.[30] Yet
at Athens there was a considerable amount of assistance for
the orphans of war and by the fourth century a system of
general payment for attendance at festivals, meetings of the
assembly, and service as jurors. As an Attic orator Demades
put it, the Theoric fund, responsible for these disbursements,
was as vital to democracy as glue to a papyrus roll.[31] Even
slaves, it may be noted, were protected by law at Athens.[32]

The inherent tension between masses and elite, described in a previous chapter, was in large measure softened at the expense of the well-to-do. One might almost wonder that they could afford luxuries, but the complaints of the Athenian rich about taxation were probably as conventional as similar murmurs in more recent ages; certainly the archeological record suggests a great increase in gold jewelry and other signs of wealth in the fourth century. So too in Victorian England the expansion of social legislation did not much diminish the revenues of Trollope's Duke of Omnium or the political power that rested on his exalted position.

Chapter 5

Cultural Role

Few aristocracies in later ages have come close to equalling the cultural activity of the upper classes of the Greek states both directly and also as patrons. The amazing outburst of Hellenic civilization in virtually every field from the eighth century onward is studded with many great names that need not be repeated here in awed litany; it will suffice to cite a few examples and more generally to consider the varied ways in which aristocrats affected contemporary arts and letters.

To begin with their literary place, Homer is as shadowy in background as in personality, but if he were a bard singing at festivals and warrior dinners such as those who appear in the epics he at least had a respected position in society. His immediate successor, Hesiod, was certainly not one of the "bribe-swallowing *basileis*" whom he scorned though he was not subservient, but from the time of Archilochus virtually every one who wrote in Greek, save the ex-slave Aesop, was either an aristocrat by birth or, as Demosthenes, of well-to-do stock.

Like Archilochus, early aristocrats were not exclusively devoted to poetry but also played their part as citizens, participating in political or military life. Alcaeus of Lesbos thus bitterly attacked Pittacus and experienced exile, as did his contemporary, Sappho, for unknown reasons. Solon, mediocre as a poet, nonetheless fired by his verse his fellow citizens to seek to regain from Megara the offshore island of Salamis and thereafter shaped on novel lines the structure of Athenian political organization. The trilogy of fifth-century Athenian tragedians is justly known for its deep meditation on the destinies of heroes, but Aeschylus wished to be remembered as a warrior and Sophocles served the state as a general. History has often in later ages been a preserve of aristocrats who also had public lives; so too the founders of Greek historiography. Herodotus, as an exile, could take no active role unless, as one tradition has it, he helped colonize Thurii, but Thucydides and Xenophon both played the role of generals.

Some early poets did make their mark primarily by celebrating the virtues of their class. Theognis of Megara was scornful and yet fearful of the *kakoi* who had gained riches without *arete*, but felt no need to be politically active or to serve as a soldier; Pindar of Thebes devoted his life to writing shimmering odes in praise of the aristocratic victors in greater or lesser contests though it should be noted that he did so in compensation for handsome pay. Before the end of the fifth century the paths of men of letters and politicians diverged from those of generals, and in the next century those who spoke in the Athenian assembly were usually of different, more upper-class origins than the generals and admirals who carried out state policy.

By this time oratory had become another significant form of Greek literature, perfected especially by Isocrates but also guided in its logical analysis by the rise of the sophists, men who professed to teach for high fees the skills needed by young aristocrats for political success. In his comedy, *The Clouds*, Aristophanes expressed the conservative opposition to their popularity, which was attended by corrosive criticism of established social and political beliefs, but the sophists were really an important ingredient in the evolution of Athenian culture. Further we need not go in tracing the evolution of Greek literature, which produced lasting models for Western civilization in poetry and prose; the source of this creativity, however, stemmed directly from aristocratic minds or at least their support as in the case of the sophists.

Among the brightest stars in the crown of Greek genius was *philosophia*, literally "love of wisdom," but more specifically an effort to understand the origins of the world and its structure as well as the place of human beings therein. In his *Theogony* Hesiod had wrestled with these problems, but he sought their motive forces on the divine plane; the philosophers were to search for purely material, natural causes. As their explorations became more evolved and complex, a side effect was the appearance of formal logic, systematic geometry, harmonics, ethical theory, and much else.

To recount here the oft-told tale of the course of Greek philosophical development is unnecessary, but it should be pointed out that the skein was stitched together purely by aristocrats in Ionia, southern Italy, and then mainland Greece. These were the men who were most likely to have the leisure to meditate on metaphysical issues; the remarkable thing is that they did so generation after generation. The first person who may be called a philosopher, Thales, in the

early sixth century was distinguished enough to urge his
fellow Ionians to unite against the Lydian threat; one of his
successors, Heraclitus, apparently could have been king (*basileus*) of Ephesus but relinquished the title, surely religious,
to his brother.[1] Pythagoras, however, who migrated from
Samos to southern Italy, was the most successful ancient
philosopher in political terms, perhaps in all times, for he
drew together a band of acolytes at Croton who dominated
the state in accordance with his ethical principles until the
other citizens grew weary of inhabiting the ancient counterpart of Calvinist Geneva.[2] As far as their origins can be
determined, all the philosophers were upper class down to
the days of Socrates, and even thereafter Plato was of blue
blood and Aristotle the cultivated son of the Macedonian
court doctor. Taken over eventually by Christianity, Greek
philosophical speculation and its methods of attack were
passed on to the modern world; even today the problems the
Greeks raised are as knotty issues as they were for the first
"thinkers" in Western history.

Whereas commoners might feel critical of the social
behavior of economic oppression by their betters, they were
far less likely to be concerned about literary changes, As
aristocrats, moreover, the authors of the Hellenic world were
not trammeled by bonds of convention either in poetic tech-
niques or in the range of their views. Early in the seventh
century Archilochus, for instance, broke with the dominance
of the hexameter in Homer, Hesiod, and the authors of the
Homeric Hymns and also boldly challenged the traditional
values of his warrior world. He thus admitted that he had
thrown away his shield in flight—"I can get another just as
good"—and in describing an ideal general favored a "bandy-
legged" fellow with feet planted on the ground and stout
of heart.[3]

More generally, poets and philosophers did have to accept criticism from their peers, a healthy sign of the vigor of Greek intellectual life. Hesiod faulted his epic predecessors for speaking "many false things as though they were true";[4] in turn the philosopher Xenophanes ruthlessly assailed Homer and Hesiod as ascribing "unto the Gods all that is reproach and blame in the world of men, stealing and adultery and deceit."[5] Solon sharply disagreed with his contemporary poet, the melancholy Mimnermus, for hoping to die at the age of sixty: "change thy song, and sing that thou art fain the fate of Death might overtake thee at fourscore," and elsewhere baldly noted that "poets tell many lies."[6]

Among the historians Hecataeus observed at the beginning of his *Genealogies*, "I write as it seems to me to be true, for the tales of the Greeks are many and [therefore] foolish."[7] In turn Herodotus criticized Hecataeus while at the same time tacitly borrowing from him, a practice not unknown among later historians. Thucydides followed by correcting two factual errors in the Father of History, though perhaps erroneously and not by name; he was more direct in attacking his contemporary Hellanicus for chronological blunders. And virtually every philosopher openly or quietly disagreed with his predecessors in the unending search for more complex and reasonable explanations of the nature of the universe.

Yet not far below the surface the standards and inherited attitudes of aristocrats had powerful, if somewhat hidden, effects on the ways poets and philosophers thought and wrote. Only once down to the fifth century, however, did some sort of public reproof seem to produce tangible results, though its sources are not clear: the poet Stesichorus, after composing a hostile *Helen*, for which he was in tradition struck blind had to reverse himself in a *Palinode*, "this was not a true tale."[8]

After 500 public, official censorship appeared more often, especially at democratic Athens, which at first sight

seems surprising in view of Pericles' assertion in the Funeral
Oration that "in our private intercourse we are not suspicious
of one another, nor angry with our neighbor if he does what
he likes."[9] The vehicle used in charges against those who
thought otherwise than the citizen body was *asebeia*,
impiety.[10]

The witchhunts that resulted sporadically in the stresses
of the Peloponnesian war were not, however, specifically directed against aristocrats save in the politically inspired trial
of Alcibiades and his cronies for parodying the Eleusinian
mysteries. The most famous case, then and in later days, was
brought in 399 against the aged Socrates, by no means a
member of the upper classes even if popular among their sons
for his insistence on finding the proper way to live despite
the danger of upsetting conventional views; the twin charges
of denying the gods of state and corrupting the youth at least
technically may have been justified.[11] It will not do to glorify
Greek civilization uncritically or to accept Pericles' noble
picture of Athenian democracy at face value.

From Hellenistic and Roman times on into the modern
period patronage was a vital link between aristocrats and
poets, philosophers, and scientists, whose views could be
shaped, even distorted, by obedience to upper-class com-
missions and preferences.[12] In classic Greece this tie did not
obtain as far as writers and philosophers were concerned; as
we have seen they were virtually all aristocrats themselves.
Artists and craftsmen on the other hand were on a different
standing. They could make objects but only if these items
were "bought" in terms of money or, before the invention
of coinage, in other ways would they be able to continue to
eat. It is very doubtful if potters, for example, "were on terms
of familiarity with the highest society in Athens,"[13] though
certainly in the days of Socrates and Plato there is abundant

reference to interchanges between philosophers and skilled laborers.[14]

In the artistic world one may begin with architects as being the most highly trained figures, though in view of their spasmodic commissioning to build temples and other public works they can scarcely be called professionals. Their pay, moreover, was not very high,[15] but they did enjoy some fame, as Rhoecus and Theodorus at Samos, Ictinus and Callicrates at Athens, and others. Ictinus himself was sought out by the Arcadians to build their temple on the wind-swept hillside at Bassae. Philon, who constructed a large arsenal at the Piraeus in the fourth century, was sufficiently proud of his edifice to describe it in a monograph and also to write a study on the proportions of temples.[16]

How far were aristocrats involved in or influential in the creation and design of temples? The evidence is at best exiguous. Initially the construction of earthly homes for the gods was probably a communal decision; certainly their erection required the use of manpower to a greater degree than any other public activity except warfare.[17] Across the seventh and sixth centuries tyrants embellished their native cities and built treasuries at Olympia, Delphi, and elsewhere, but the choice of subject for sculptural decoration seems more patriotic than personal; celebration of a tyrant's life and achievements was more likely to appear in objects dedicated in the shrines, such as the chest in which the infant Cypselus was hidden. Late in the sixth century the Alcmeonid family secured the contract for rebuilding the temple of Apollo at Delphi, destroyed by fire, but at least for the Alcmeonids themselves the fruits were principally the gain of Spartan support against the tyrant Hippias.

Eventually larger states took over control of public works. At Athens the first step in a new edifice was an en-

abling decree by the assembly; that for Philon's arsenal was
so detailed in specific terms that the building can be recon-
structed even though none of it physically survives at the
harbor of Zea.[18] Building commissioners (*neopoioi* or the like)
were appointed who, with the city architect (elected for ex-
pertise, not appointed by lot), made final decisions, let contracts, and supervised the ensuing construction.[19] Expenses
were carefully watched and recorded on stone at Athens,
Eleusis, Epidaurus, Delphi and elsewhere down to the amount
spent on repair of a slave's sandals, and even the most minute
matters could be regulated by decrees of the Athenian assembly, which thus legislated on the details of the door of the
temple of Athena Nike.[20]

Probably the commissioners were aristocrats, like Pericles for the Parthenon, or at least well-to-do, but as in the
age of tyrants there is little suggestion in the sculptural
decoration of temples of aristocratic influence on the choice of
subject or manner of execution. If the Parthenon frieze celebrated noble maidens and youths in the Panathenaic procession, this was a civic affair; so too in the painting depicting
Marathon in the Stoa Poikile historical figures such as the
polemarch Callimachus, Miltiades, and others appeared as
heroes of the battle against the Persians, not for their aristocratic status. Where aristocratic attitudes might show
themselves was in the construction of rural shrines and other
private buildings such as the little temple of Athena Aris-
toboule (of best council) which Themistocles built near his
own home, but material of this type has not survived in any
useful measure.

Pottery was produced in smaller dimensions than buildings and on a personal level. The large kraters and amphoras
that crowned the Dipylon graves of the well-to-do in the
eighth century were certainly commissioned pieces, and their
figured scenes of funeral processions and battles by sea, though

impersonal in style, must reflect the wishes of the deceased or of his relatives. Thereafter, across the seventh and sixth centuries, the products of Athenian workshops were turned out in ever greater amounts for general Mediterranean sale.[21] At least one type of vase, however, which was made from 550 to 450 depicted a handsome Athenian young noble labeled "Leagros kalos" or the like or simply *ho pais kalos* (beautiful boy); over 200 figures are thus known, aimed surely primarily at the Agora market.[22] *Kalos* cups, even so, survive in such numbers and turn up as far as Etruria that direct commissioning does not appear very likely. Although Athenian vases cost far less than one might expect (or is true in modern markets), they must still have largely been purchased by those with long purses even if their makers were sufficiently independent in standing to place their own dedications on the Acropolis.

So too jewelers, perfumers, and makers of bronze candelabra and fine furniture worked primarily for an audience of wealth, but on the other hand the customers had to depend on these skilled artisans to secure their products; the symbiosis between patron and artist must have been close. As for the important field of artistic output, free-standing sculpture, less can be said on mutual relationships than one would wish.[23] Assuredly the statues of noble maidens (*korai*) and youths (*kouroi*), which were dedicated on the Acropolis, placed on graves, and otherwise distributed over the Attic countryside in the sixth century as well as the relief tombstones of the Kerameikos were specifically commissioned, but though they reflect publicly, without reserve, an aristocratic ethos they do not depict in tangible detail the attitudes we find in the poets of the age and in the later works of Plato and Aristotle.[24]

On the whole, in sum, the artists of Greece could not have exhibited that unceasing search for perfection in ever-developing styles without the support of aristocratic patrons, though it must be emphasized again that unlike poets and philosophers they were not themselves of upper-class lineage. If the artistic traditions of Hellenic civilization inspired first Rome and then generally from the Renaissance on fascinated the Western world down to the present day we are once more heavily indebted to the aristocrats who dominated and shaped the ancient Greek *polis* world.

Chapter 6

Gods and Priests

In the novels of Anthony Trollope the clergy and the administrators of the Church of England are almost entirely gentlemen, usually educated at Oxford or Cambridge, living well but often without much concern for their religious duties; even so they directed a tightly organized structure that sternly demanded moral, social, and political obedience to the established order. In France and other European countries as well the church was a principal aide of the state in providing an "opiate for the masses"; it is small wonder that in times of upheaval—the English Civil Wars, the French and Russian revolutions, and elsewhere—that local religious systems and their personnel were savagely attacked and often extirpated.

Religion in classic Greece was of a very different order. There was no Saint Peter standing at the gates of Heaven to judge the worthiness of dead souls; instead gloomy Charon rowed his charges across the river Styx to a shadowy Hades— "better is it," burst out Achilles in the *Odyssey*, "to be a landless peasant on earth than a king among the dead."[1] Greek religion, however, was directly tied to public life. In a *polis*, Aristotle firmly stated, the first responsibility "in order of merit . . . is an establishment for the service of the gods or, as it is called, public worship."[2] Even in classic Athens religious business was the first item on the agenda of several meetings of the assembly, and a mark of citizenship was the right to participate in worship of Athena on the Acropolis. As a later law of Paros ordained, "It is not lawful for a Doric stranger or a slave to be a spectator of the rites of Kore of the Polis."[3]

On this level, an eminent student has summed up the situation:

> Seen from without, traditional Greek religion has all the marks of a social phenomenon, a thing which concerns the state. Temples are dedicated to the civic gods. Priests are civic magistrates. On certain days all the citizens, in a body, men, women, and children, gather before the temple for a solemn sacrifice. The hymns then sung in honor of the god, the prayers addressed to him, have an official character; it is a matter of obtaining the god's favor for the prosperity and well-being of the entire people.[4]

In the foundation of colonies not only was the advice of Apollo sought at Delphi, but proper transfer of the cults of the mother city to the offshoot was vital. Rather than being an opiate, Greek religion was thus a cement for society, and the protection of divine spirits stretched so far as to safeguard even potters from evil forces that might endanger their products.[5]

What has all this to do with aristocrats? A great deal, more than in Trollope's England, for the upper classes essentially established the way the Greeks visualized their gods and also the structure of worship. The nature of the heavenly pantheon, as Xenophanes angrily observed, had been firmly set by Homer and Hesiod. Both, to be sure, lived before that consolidation of the aristocratic pattern that we have examined in preceding pages, but Xenophanes' outburst that they ascribed "unto the Gods all that is reproach and blame in the world of men, stealing and adultery and deceit," directly reflected the scarcely civilized concepts of the warrior heroes who fought at Troy.[6] In other fragments Xenophanes attacked the anthropomorphic views of deity—"the Aethiopian says that the Gods are snub-nosed and black, the Thracian that his have blue eyes and red hair"—and repeatedly denied that mortal men could ever know the truth about the gods.[7] Yet his fellow citizens then and later refused to abandon their picture of deities as many and as undying, superhuman figures in human shape. By the eighth century they were erecting temples to house statues that eventually attained canonical form so that a modern student of Greek art can easily identify Athena with her helmet or Zeus with his thunderbolt, both like the other gods essentially visualized in aristocratic shape.

As the Greek world, however, becme more civilized, so too did its gods. Even in the epics, especially the *Odyssey*, there is occasional suggestion that Zeus favored justice; Hesiod firmly believed that the Father of the Gods punished crooked judgments of contemporary *basileis* by famine, plague, lack of children, and destruction at home and on the sea.[8] Thus far, however, the responsibility for earthly justice was in the hands of Zeus; there was not yet any idea that men by their own actions can secure or restore justice to a community. By the time of Solon Greek thought had advanced to a stage that asserted human beings had such an influence; evil events in the state, the Athenian reformer preached, were the product of ignorance by the common citizen even if the well-to-do might be the leaders in securing *eunomia*. "The common evil comes into every house, and the street door will no longer keep it out; it leaps the high hedge and surely finds one, for all he may go hide himself in his chamber."[9] Thenceforth Athenian public life came more and more to be based on the premise that citizens had both duties and rights, safeguarded by secular sanctions more than by divine protection.

The administration and operation of Greek religious machinery everywhere continued to be largely the preserve of local aristocrats; here perhaps more than in any other aspect of Hellenic life inherited customs had heavy weight. The Homeric *basileus* usually approached the gods and with the aid of seers obtained divine guidance. These functions in the historic *poleis* were the province of priests who were, as already noted, far more civil servants than religiously dedicated individuals; at times they were appointed or otherwise served by inheritance.

To consider only Athens, which is best illuminated in our sources, the formal head of its religious structure was the king archon, who by custom and then by law had to be an aristocrat; perhaps the gods would listen only when addressed by a *basileus* of proper standing. Each year the sacred wooden image of Athena was escorted to the seacoast at Phalerum for its bath under the direction of the family of the Praxiergidae; the Panathenaic procession was led by the *kanephoroi* (basket bearers as depicted on the Parthenon frieze), maidens of high birth with both parents living.[10] Many ancestral cults of importance were in the hands of aristocratic families, such as those that administered the Eleusinian mysteries and shrines dotted about the Attic landscape that focused and maintained local pride and attachment.[11]

Influenced no doubt by the employment of religious systems for aristocratic ends in modern times, some scholars have sought to discover in archaic and classical Greece a similar pattern, but the very different nature of Hellenic religious beliefs must leave one wary of assuming that upper-class priests even of inherited status could often transform their positions into dangerous political power.[12] Their role was very much that of civil servants, and as such they were scarcely able, unlike bishops and abbots in medieval and early modern Europe, to convert religious economic resources to their own ends. As the great Swedish student of Greek religion, Nilsson, observed, "From early times Greek religion was bound to the state and to society; these three constituted an unbreakable unity. There was no profession of priesthoods, whose interests could come into conflict with society and the state."[13] If anything, the limitations went the other way; from early historical times onward aristocratic self-assertion in funeral pomp was restricted in many states.[14]

An unusual problem that does surface from time to time at Athens is the fact that a rootless part of society, that is, those without ancestors or relatives attached to local cults, needed to be integrated religiously in the body politic when it was reformed in a more democratic or popular fashion. Among Solon's laws there was one that apparently admitted this element into cult groups, and evidence exists at Cyrene and Argos for similar steps.[15] The Athenian reformer Cleisthenes, however, went no further than to allow "everybody retain his family connections, his membership in a brotherhood, and his family rites according to ancestral custom."[16]

Thereafter, across the fifth and fourth centuries, the Athenian assembly at times passed decrees regulating cult, sacrifices, and the erection of temples, but there was no need to "break" an aristocratic domination of religion as a whole so as to eliminate a political threat therefrom. Commoners

were generally happy to let the machinery of sacrifice and
other aspects of cult be conducted on their behalf by their
betters; to judge from the decline of dedications to Athena
on the Acropolis her figure receded farther and farther from
popular interest.[17]

Almost entirely outside the established forms of religious activity there did appear in the archaic and classical era
a number of ecstatic cults centered in part on Dionysus, which
the state viewed with suspicion as leading to undisciplined
behavior and tried to bring into more ordered forms of worship; even more personal and unfettered was the rise of mag-
ical practices that involved, for example, burying curses
inscribed on lead plates and an abundance of dedications of
clay figurines at shrines which protected especially women in
their manifold physical problems.

We must not, to repeat an earlier warning, idealize the
Greeks too far. What can only be called superstition continued to produce rituals for the phenomena of menstruation,
childbirth, and other upsetting aspects of life.[18] The Greeks
in early times had been as primitive as any people studied
by modern anthropologists and dragged with them into the
historical era much of their ancestral inheritance; the important fact is that they did not allow their advance to be
checked by taboos.

Over all stood the magnificent figures of the great gods,
visualized largely in aristocratic mien and attended by the
rich mythological dress spun by Greek imagination, wor-
shipped in formal procedures conducted by priests and pries-
tesses of upper-class origins. When the industrious traveler
Pausanias came to Athens in the second century after Christ
he was so impressed by its continuing religious observances
as to exclaim, "The Athenians are far more dedicated to
religion than other men."[19]

Chapter 7

The Afterlife
of Greek Aristocracy

After Alexander's conquest of the Persian empire 334–323
B.C. Greek civilization broadened out to encompass all the
eastern Mediterranean. This new era has been given in modern
times the unhappy term "Hellenistic," Greek-like but not
exactly the same as classical Hellenism. Now poets, artists,
even philosophers were subsidized, not by aristocrats, but by
the kings of Egypt, Syria, and other states and often obse-
quiously celebrated the virtues of their royal patrons. In literature elegant "Alexandrian" conceits and the exploitation
of obscure local legends were the province of professional,
learned scholars; in the arts urbane, cosmopolitan artistic
types and styles, such as nude Venuses and figures expressing

violent emotion, were to be very popular in Rome and then in modern Western Europe.

Their work, however, was framed within the social, cultural, even religious matrix inherited directly from classical Greece. Although aristocrats might lose political power first to Macedon and then eventually to Rome, they remained locally potent. Throughout the fourth century social unrest had been a curse in Greece, spurred by the battle cry "abolition of debts and redivision of the land," a slogan that continued to produce upheavals and civil war in the Hellenistic period. Even so, as is often the case, the rich got richer and flaunted their wealth in ever more luxurious houses adorned with floor mosaics and frescoed walls as well as a greater abundance of gold jewelry. At Athens, where our evidence is again most abundant, aristocrats varied from time to time in political power but continued to be active and to pass on their role through *gene* or clans, artificial constructs that now were widely accepted;[1] one family can thus be followed in public life over nine generations.

The cities of Asia Minor and the new urban centers created from the time of Alexander onward were more directly controlled by the kings but usually enjoyed local autonomy; they were vital in maintaining order in the countryside and were valuable conduits for the taxable cash that flowed through their markets and ports. Here, if anywhere in the ancient world, one might almost speak of a bourgeois outlook, for the well-to-do lived on invested capital in land, shops, stores, slaves—selfish and materialistic, aiming at a quiet life with a minimum of worry, requirements that were largely met by the new Stoic and Epicurean philosophies, not much given to urging social reform.[2] Eventually their royal masters were wiped out by the ruthless advance of Roman power, but the leaders of the urban centers survived under Roman rule for centuries and remained attached to their communities. Plutarch could boast of knowing a direct descendant of Themistocles, who still enjoyed ancestral revenues at Magnesia; about A.D. 200 one leader of the young men of Athens, the ephebes, urged his charges to keep as an example the legendary deeds of Theseus.[3]

"Captive Greece took captive its uncivilized conqueror," ran a jingle in one of Horace's poems.[4] He might have been thinking of events in the Hellenistic age, but actually the influence of Greek civilization, attested physically by pottery imports, ran far back in Roman history to the period of Etruscan domination. The city of Rome itself put on an urban dress of temples and other public buildings by the sixth century; it is too often overlooked that the Roman Forum was regularized as early as was the Athenian *agora*. True, Rome and Italy lay in a backwater in the great days of fifth-century Greek arts and letters, but at least by the beginning of the fourth century ties between Rome and the Greek world became more extensive and varied. Rome thus dedicated a gold bowl at Delphi after its destruction of Veii in 396; toward the end of the century statues were erected in the Forum to Pythagoras and, oddly enough, to Alcibiades as the result of seeking advice from the Delphic oracle.

Basing himself on the statement that Roman ambassadors to Tarentum spoke Greek, Mommsen concluded that young Roman aristocrats "acquired a knowledge of what was to be the general language of the world in diplomacy,"[5] and though this may predate widespread Roman knowledge of Greek, certainly the great aristocrat and statesman, Appius Claudius, early in the third century composed a work of proverbs, the *Sententiae*, in the local Saturnian verse but indebted to Greek sources; the learned Greek philosopher, Panaetius, was later to be able to praise it. Before the end of this century the composition of history at Rome had begun in the work of Fabius Pictor, written in Greek. Even more remarkable is the fact that Roman aristocrats of political importance, such as Q. Publilius Philo, consul four times from 339 and also dictator, and several later political leaders had or adopted Greek cognomina.[6] The famous bust of "Brutus" in the Capitoline Museum, perhaps of this period, shows a haughty aristocrat with cold, reserved stare.[7] The perfected form of Ciceronian prose and Virgilian poetry was a long process; so too no doubt the refinement of Roman aristocratic ways extended down into the last century B.C., when men like Cicero and Caesar completed their education by studying in the Aegean with Greek philosophers and rhetoricians. One can only wonder if their mentors found the Roman pupils as naive yet vigorous as have European teachers of American students in recent generations.[8]

By this time the leaders of Rome had long since abandoned the simple ways of their idealized ancestors who "esteemed" in the words of Livy's preface, "thrift and plain living." The wealth of growing empire as Roman armies ransacked the Hellenistic East permitted an outburst of luxury scarcely equalled in all ancient history. Those who lived in the great mansions on the Palatine hill also wholeheartedly adopted Greek aristocratic principles, repeated in Latin dress especially in the essays of Cicero. Roman culture was deeply stamped as Republic yielded to Empire in the days of Augustus; eventually in early modern times, as we shall see shortly, Roman aristocratic models were to reenforce their Greek prototypes.

Across the long centuries of the Roman Empire fundamental changes took place in people's views of their place in the world and the rule of the divine, marked most noticeably but not exclusively in the victory of Christianity. Elsewhere I have analyzed how these changes, which broke the bonds of classical civilization, were vital for the rise of a new world outlook, but immediately they were as devastating as the collapse of the Roman empire in the West and the Germanic conquests.[9] Among the losses was the disappearance of the aristocratic way of life; after the last flickers in the work of Cassiodorus and Sidonius Apollinaris one seeks in vain for any conscious, significant survival of the concept of aristocracy until well after A.D. 1000. It is true that in the *Song of Roland* there is reference to the "gentil home" (man) of the Franks, and in Chaucer's *Romaunt of the Rose* Love proclaims a gentle man is not the product of birth but of virtue, yet a full-blown revival of attention to aristocratic superiority came only in the fifteenth century in the Italian Renaissance and its reflections in France, England, and elsewhere.[10]

A consideration here of the resuscitation of aristocratic attitudes must be limited in detail lest I stray too far from the areas of my own special knowledge. Helpful guidance, however, has been provided by a number of excellent studies by modern historians, and the swiftness with which the Western world resumed an aristocratic dress suggests the power of the inheritance. Especially in Italy scholars were again acquainted with Plato, particularly the *Republic*, and also Aristotle's *Nicomachean Ethics*, translated into Latin in 1414 by Bruni and published in its Greek text at Venice in 1508.

Based on these treatises as well as Theophrastus' *Characters*, Giovanni della Casa wrote his *Galateo*, published in 1558 and soon translated into French, which has been well described as "a modern code of good manners, which has received no major alterations from the sixteenth century to our own day."[11] Even more influential was Baldassare Castiglione, *Il Cortegiano*, published in 1528 in Italian, in 1537 in French, and in English in 1561. As Barker observed, "His conception of culture became the general European ideal (coloured, it is true, in each country by something of a national tincture)."[12]

Thenceforth a clearly defined aristocratic code had become standard in all the courts of western Europe and was widely accepted by the upper classes or gentry focused in the principal universities.[13] Aristocracy unfortunately was a formal concept that lacked the fructifying powers of its Greek source; while accepted usually by their inferiors aristocrats were not widely praised in literature from the Renaissance onward, and certainly by the nineteenth and twentieth centuries have often been savagely attacked as useless parasites on society. Even in the Renaissance itself Machiavelli had condemned "those who live in idleness on the abundant resources of their estates."[14]

Yet these assaults must not disguise the powerful effects of the Greek inheritance as mediated at time through Rome. Writers of prose down through Gibbon, Macaulay, and their contemporaries in other countries followed the models provided by Isocrates and Cicero; poets, including Milton and many others, were heavily influenced by Alexandrian and Virgilian sources. In the arts painters loved to depict classical historical and mythological scenes; their confreres in sculpture knew at least from the days of Winckelmann that classical works such as the Laocoon were almost beyond imitation, but the effort was made by Canova and others. Only in the nascent sciences was ancient inspiration of limited effect, and even so Euclid's *Elements*, perhaps the most influential textbook ever written, was not seriously challenged until the twentieth century.

To return to a Victorian novelist whose characters have appeared at several points in these pages, Trollope in one of his minor works, *Ralph the Heir*, graphically and succinctly illustrates the many differences in ways of life between aristocrats and commoners. Ontario Moggs, son of a bootmaker, is in love with Polly Neefit, daughter of a very successful tailor of gentlemen's riding breeches, but alas Ralph, a gentleman, also seeks Polly's hand. "With all his scorn for gentry Ontario Moggs in his heart feared a gentleman. He thought that he could make an effort to punch Ralph Newton's head if they were ever to be brought together in a spot convenient for such an operation; but of the man's standing in the world, he was afraid. It seemed to him to be impossible that Polly should prefer him, or any one of his class, to a suitor whose hands were always clean, whose shirt was always white, whose words were soft and well-chosen, who carried with him none of the stain of work . . . of himself, who was a man of the people, and a tradesman, he thought very little when he compared himself to a gentleman. He could not speak as they spoke; he could not walk as they walked; he could not eat as they ate."[15] The aristocrats who lived in the age of Aristotle would have nodded assent to his self-depreciation, but we may note that Polly is aware that she is not a lady and in the end takes Ontario.

Trollope, like G. M. Trevelyan in an earlier chapter, may be dismissed as an elitist, the easy way out for coping with unpopular views, but I for one am far from convinced that the Western world has entirely overpassed and forgotten its inheritance. In *My Fair Lady* Professor Henry Higgins bursts out in irritation at the corruption of English in Covent Gardens, "An Englishman's way of speaking absolutely classifics him . . . This verbal class distinction by now should be antique." But is it?

There is, indeed, one geographical area that has obstinately denied aristocratic influence in mode of life, though not in arts and letters. Citizens of the United States know that they are not aristocrats, nor were their American ancestors; if asked they would triumphantly, if at all possible, proclaim themselves "middle class." The answer is a bit deceptive. Earlier we noted an American of ancestral lineage who put birth ahead of wealth; in a recent review of a biography of

Henry Stimson the critic observed, "Born to wealth, educated at Andover, Yale College, and Harvard Law School, Stimson easily assumed his place in what passed for the American aristocracy in the late Gilded Age."[16] The ambiguous wording reflects the deeply treasured opinion that no American *can* be an aristocrat, though the reserved, aloof figure of Stimson over many years suggests the truth lies elsewhere.

To return finally to the problem posed in my introduction, Greek aristocracy had a vital role in many aspects of the amazing development of Hellenic civilization which I have sought to illustrate in some detail in discussing its political, social, economic, cultural, and religious role once the aristocratic ethos had been consolidated. Its influence, as I have suggested briefly in this concluding chapter, did not end when ancient civilization flickered out but was reborn in the Renaissance; thereafter it has had powerful effects in the course of modern Western history.

Notes

INTRODUCTION

1. London: Chatto and Windus, 1980). See also the collection of essays and full bibliography in his *Economy and Society in Ancient Greece*, ed. B. D. Shaw and R. P. Saller (London, 1981). A thorough study was published by G. E. M. de Ste Croix, *The Class Struggle in the Ancient Greek World* (Ithaca, 1981), which unfortunately was hampered by Marxist blinkers. An extended report on European work may be found in N. Brockmeyer, *Antike Sklaverei* (Darmstadt, 1979). Finley and I were friends for many years but tacitly agreed to differ on slavery; my point of view was set forth in "An Overdose of Slavery," *Journal of Economic History*

18 (1958), pp. 17–32 (now in my *Essays on Ancient History*, ed. A. Ferrill and T. Kelly [Leiden, 1979], pp. 43–58), an essay which as far as I am aware has been appreciated only by E. Badian, *The Craft of the Ancient Historian: Essays in Honor of Chester G. Starr*, ed. J. W. Eadie and J. Ober (Lanham, Md., 1985), pp. 13–14.

2. L. Whibley, *Greek Oligarchies: Their Character and Organisation* (London, 1896); a more recent study by M. T. W. Arnheim, *Aristocracy in Greek Society* (New York, 1977), must be mentioned though it is unimaginative and an inadequate treatment of the subject.

CHAPTER 1

1. *Iliad* 2. 212ff. Beauty: *Odyssey* 4. 62–64, 13. 223, 18. 217–19.

2. A. W. H. Adkins, *Merit and Responsibility* (Oxford, 1960), p. 34. The distinction I would stress may be found also in G. M. Calhoun, "Classes and Masses in Homer," *Classical Philology* 29 (1934), pp. 192–208, and H. Strasburger, "Der soziologische Aspekt der homerischen Epen," *Gymnasium* 60 (1953), pp. 97–114.

3. O. Murray, *The Greek Renaissance of the Eighth Century B. C.* ed. R. Hägg (Stockholm, 1983), p. 195. In a number of essays and especially *The Aristocratic Ideal in Archaic Greece* (Lawrence, Kansas, 1980), W. Donlan provides very useful guidance to the range of literary evidence.

4. I have considered this change in greater detail in "Decline of the Early Greek Kings," *Historia* 10 (1961), pp. 129–38 (now in my *Essays on Ancient History*, pp. 134–43). Whibley, *Greek Oligarchies*, pp. 68–72, is brief but thoughtful.

5. Alcaeus fr. Z 103; or more tersely Thucydides 7. 77, "men are the *polis*." The estimates of wealth and population by L. Nixon and S. Price in *The Greek City from Homer to Alexander* (New York, 1990), pp. 137ff., are not very useful; the figures in my

text come from E. Ruschenbusch, *Untersuchungen zu Staat und Politik in Griechenland vom 7.–4 Jh. v. Chr.* (Bamberg, 1978), pp. 4ff.

6. E. R. Service, *Origins of the State and Civilization* (Philadelphia, 1978), p. 8.

7. In *Individual and Community: The Rise of the Polis 800–500 B.C.* (New York, 1986), pp. 34–51, I have sought to demonstrate the conditions under which the *polis* emerged.

8. As Julius Gerlach, *Aner Agathos* (Diss. Munich, 1932), showed, that term did not yet have a class significance in the seventh century; in Homer and even in Archilochus bravery and beauty do not necessarily go hand in hand (*Iliad* 5. 801, 787).

9. Plutarch, *Nob.* 2 (ed. Bernadakis 8); *Odyssey* 4. 62–64; Archilochus fr. 195 (cf. fr. 65).

10. Sappho fr. 155; A. E. Raubitschek, *Dedications from the Athenian Acropolis* (Cambridge, Mass., 1949), pp. 464–67, is thoughtful on the difficulty of distinguishing aristocrats in our epigraphic evidence due to the lack of titles.

11. Stobaeus, *Anthologium* 4. 29 (86. 25) = Aristotle fr. 92 Rose (cf. *Politics* 5. 1. 1301b); Aristotle, *Constitution of Athens* 3. The sentiment was repeated by Lord Burleigh, "Gentilitie is naught but ancient riches" (Roy Perrott, *The Aristocrats* [London, 1968], p. 256); it is fascinating to find that even in twentieth-century America an aristocrat of venerable lineage can observe, "Time or wealth. Which is more important in people's perception of class? There has to have been wealth, but it's time mostly" (Nelson Aldrich, *Fortune* June 30, 1990, p. 124).

12. J. K. Davies, *Athenian Propertied Families 600–300 B. C.* (Oxford, 1971), pp. xxff., though these later trierarchs were not necessarily landed aristocrats; Polybius 12. 5. 6. On the hectare estimates see my *Economic and Social Growth of Early Greece, 800–500 B. C.* (New York, 1977), pp. 153–55.

13. M. K. Langdon, *American Journal of Archaeology* 79 (1975), pp. 139–40.

14. P. Walcot, *Greek Peasants, Ancient and Modern* (Manchester, 1971), and *Hesiod and the Near East* (Cardiff, 1966), gives the conventional view; C. A. Roebuck, *Trade and Politics in the*

Ancient World, ed. M. I. Finley (Paris/Hague, 1965), p. 100, calls him "a substantial free-holding farmer," which is closer to the mark. See briefly *Economic and Social Growth of Early Greece, 800– 500 B. C.*, pp. 126–27.

15. *Works and Days* 589.

16. As Adkins does in *Merit and Responsibility* and *Moral Values*; contra, my *Origins of Greek Civilization 1100–650 B. C.* (New York, 1961), pp. 272–75, 295–98, 343–45; it is also possible that later Greeks selected from the work of Archilochus passages that best expressed his relative modernity.

17. Archilochus fr. 115–16, 118.

18. E. Barker, *Traditions of Civility* (Cambridge, 1948), p. 126; W. L. Wiley, *The Gentleman of Renaissance France* (Cambridge, Mass., 1954), pp. 28–29.

19. Mimnermus fr. 7; Hesiod's diatribe against bribe-swallowing *basileis* may be accounted in the same vein.

CHAPTER 2

1. Wiley, *The Gentleman of Renaissance France*, gives a rounded picture of the role of aristocrats at that time; consider also the depiction of Persian and Mede courtiers on the staircases of the Apadana at Persepolis.

2. *Politics* 1. 2 1253a; 3. 6 1279a, 1. 12 1259b, 4. 11 1295b, and elsewhere.

3. *Politics* 4. 8 1293b; 1. 13 1260a, 3. 13 1284a.

4. *Politics* 4. 1 1288b.

5. *Politics* 3. 15 1286b.

6. *Politics* 5. 1302b; interestingly enough Plato in the *Politicus* judged democracy the best of all "bad forms" of government.

7. *Politics* 3. 1 1275a–b.

8. *Politics* 4. 11 1295b–96a.

9. *Odyssey* 7. 310; Hesiod, *Works and Days* 694.

10. *Suppliants* 238ff., cf. Pindar, *Pythian Odes* 11. 50–53.

11. I have treated briefly *to meson* in *Individual and Community*, pp. 96–97, with references to modern views.

12. Aristotle, *Politics* 3. 15 1286b.

13. Solon's reforms are sketched in *Individual and Community*, pp. 77–80, again with reference to modern literature.

14. H. Bolkestein, *Economic Life in Greece's Golden Age* (Leiden, 1958), pp. 140–41; W. Kendrick Pritchett, *Ancient Greek Military Practices*, 1 (Berkeley, 1971), pp. 93–100.

15. Especially *Politics* 4. 13 1297b; cf. my *Individual and Community*, pp. 80–81, and A. Andrewes, *The Greek Tyrants* (London, 1956).

16. Heracleides Ponticus, in *Fragmenta Historicorum Graecorum*, ed. K. Müller, 2 (Paris, 1878), p. 217; Strabo 10. 447; Herodotus 5. 77; cf. Aristotle, *Politics* 4. 3 1289b.

17. Herodotus 1. 153.

18. Phocylides fr. 6 (Diehl); Hesiod, *Works and Days* 477–48, 349–51; as M. Sahlins, *Stone Age Economics* (London, 1974), pp. 217–18, observes, food in simple societies is given or shared; "food has too much social value . . . to have exchange value." This altered greatly in the era of Greek expansion.

19. G. Mingay, *The Gentry* (London, 1976); E. Wingfield-Stratton, *The Squire and His Relations* (London, 1956).

20. S. I. Oost, "The Megara of Theagenes and Theognis," *Classical Philology* 68 (1973), pp. 186–96; G. Cerri, "La terminologia sociopolitica di Theognide," *Quaderni Urbinati* 6 (1968), pp. 7–32; more generally M. L. West, *Studies in Greek Elegy and Iambus* (Berlin, 1974), chaps. 3 and 4.

21. Theognis 847–50; W. Donlon, *Parola del Passato* 25 (1970), p. 393.

22. Donlan, *Aristocratic Ideal in Archaic Greece*, p. 77.

23. Herodotus 5. 66.

24. See for the following discussion my *Birth of Athenian Democracy: The Assembly in the Fifth Century* (New York, 1990).

25. Davies, *Athenian Propertied Families*, pp. 348ff.; S. Humphreys, "Lycurgus of Butadae: An Athenian Aristocrat," *Craft of the Ancient Historian*, pp. 199–252.

26. E. Badian, *Zeitschrift für Papyrologie und Epigraphik* 79 (1989), p. 62.

27. J. Ober, *Mass and Elite in Democratic Athens* (Princeton, 1989).

28. Whibley, *Greek Oligarchies*, pp. 72–83, well describes this shift from aristocracy to oligarchy, and on pp. 105ff. properly observes that oligarchy and aristocracy continued to be interwoven in Greek political life and theory.

29. Whibley, pp. 139–91, gives a detailed account of the diversity of oligarchic constitutions. Aristotle, *Politics* 4. 9 1294b contrasts democratic choice by lot and oligarchic preference for votes.

30. Whibley, p. 191.

31. *Politics* 5. 8 1309a, 2. 7 1266b and elsewhere especially in book 5.

CHAPTER 3

1. M. L. Bush, *The European Nobility*, 2 (Manchester, 1988), as noted in *American Historical Review* 95 (1990), p. 809.

2. Plato, *Protagoras* 347 c–d.

3. The bourgeoisie does not come off much better than aristocracy these days; for a level-headed appreciation of the bourgeois state of mind see T. Zeldin, *France 1848–1945* (Oxford, 1973), pp. 11ff.

4. F. Braudel, *Capitalism and Material Life 1400–1800* (New York, 1973), p. 122.

5. J. Pollard, *Journal of Hellenic Studies* 93 (1973), p. 221.

6. Horos 14 in M. I. Finley, *Studies in Land and Credit in Ancient Athens 500–200 B. C.* (New Brunswick, N. J., 1952),

lists a house and plot (rural) and a "house in the city" from the late fourth century.

7. Sappho fr. 57.

8. F. Bourriot, *Recherches sur la nature du genos* (Paris, 1976); see also D. Roussel, *Tribu et cité* (Paris, 1976)—but the concept is too useful to be discarded even if disproved.

9. D. Asheri, *Distribuzioni di terre nell'antica Grecia*, Memorie dell' Accademia delle scienze di Torino, classe di scienze morale, storiche e filologiche, 4 ser. 10 (1966), p. 9.

10. Cf. J. P. Vernant, "Le mariage en Grèce archaïque," *Parola del Passato* 28 (1973), pp. 51–74; Hesiod, *Works and Days* 702–704.

11. See generally Davies, *Athenian Propertied Families*.

12. D. L. Page, *Sappho and Alcaeus* (Oxford, 1955), pp. 170–71; the most recent treatment of guest friendship is G. Herman, *Ritualised Friendship and the Greek City* (Cambridge, 1987).

13. Solon fr. 13.

14. *Politics* 7. 8 1329a.

15. Herodotus 1. 30; cf. Callinus, Tyrtaeus fr. 4, 7, Mimnermus fr. 13, and other archaic voices.

16. At Athens, however, the maximum fee was two drachmas, the only example known of wage-fixing; see generally my essay, "An Evening with the Flute Girls," *Parola del Passato* 33 (1978), pp. 401–10.

17. *Symposium* 2. 1; in the Decretals of Gregory IX, a scene reproduced in G. M. Trevelyan, *Illustrated English Social History*, 1 (Pelican, 1964), no. 72 exactly the same pattern of entertainers from the fourteenth century appears.

18. J. Henderson, *The Maculate Muse* (New Haven, 1975), p. 81.

19. Cf. the thoughtful remarks of O. Murray, *The Greek Renaissance of the Eighth Century B. C.*, ed. R. Hägg (Stockholm, 1983), pp. 195–99; on the *andron* M. H. Jameson, *The Greek City from Homer to Alexander*, pp. 188–91; and on collective activities as a whole P. Schmitt-Pantel in the same volume, pp. 199–213.

20. British Museum B 421 (J. Boardman, *Athenian Black*

84 Notes

Figure Vases [London, 1974]), fig. 110; cf. H. G. Buchholz, G. Jährens, K. Maull, *Jagd und Fischfang* (*Archaeologia Homerica*, 2, part J [Göttingen, 1973]).

21. H. W. Pleket, "Zur Soziologie des antiken Sports," *Mededelingen van het Nederlands Instituut te Rome*, 36 (1974), pp. 57–87.

22. G. Pugliese Carratelli, *Atti e Memorie della Società Magna Graecia*, n. s. 6 (1965), pp. 13–17, as cited by Pleket, p. 67.

23. Isocrates 16. 33; parallels to English fox-hunting and racing will easily come to mind.

24. Semonides fr. 7; see my *Economic and Social Growth*, pp. 131–33.

25. Until fairly recently the most useful study of Greek homosexuality was E. Bethe, "Die dorische Knabenliebe," *Rheinisches Museum*, 62 (1907), pp. 438–75, even if erroneous in title; but one can now turn to K. Dover, *Greek Homosexuality* (London, 1978), and other monographs.

26. So on Lesbos (Alcaeus fr. 130); see generally S. B. Pomeroy, *Goddesses, Whores, Wives and Slaves* (New York, 1978), chap. 3, and also the thoughtful exploration by D. M. Schaps, *Economic Rights of Women in Ancient Greece* (Edinburgh, 1979).

27. See generally D. C. Kurtz and J. Boardman, *Greek Burial Customs* (Ithaca, 1971); I. Morris, *Burial and Ancient Society: The Rise of the Greek City-state* (New York, 1987), is an interesting search for political and social change as reflected in Greek graves (as in the rise of the *kakoi*).

28. The following bear almost exclusively on the classical period and are unfavorable to elites: R. R. Bolgar in R. Wilkinson, ed., *Governing Elites* (New York, 1966), pp. 23–49; R. Seager in F. C. Jaher, ed., *The Rich, The Well Born and the Powerful* (Urbana, Ill., 1973), pp. 7–26; E. C. Welskopf, "Elitevorstellungen und Elitebildung in der hellenischen Polis," *Klio* 43–45 (1965), pp. 49–64. H. I. Marrou, *History of Education in Antiquity* (New York, 1956), pp. 5–13, is more objective; for an early modern parallel see M. Motley, *Becoming a French Aristocrat: The Education of the Court Nobility, 1580–1715* (Princeton, 1990).

29. *Odyssey* 8. 236ff.; Xenophanes fr. 3; Athenaeus 12. 525f.
30. Thucydides 1. 6.
31. Alcman fr. 33; Hipponax fr. 39.
32. See my *Economic and Social Growth*, pp. 41–42.
33. S. Laser, *Hausrat* (Archaeologia Homerica, 2, part P [Göttingen, 1968]); on Athenian houses see J. Travlos, *Pictorial Dictionary of Ancient Athens* (London, 1971), *s. v. oikia.*
34. H. Troyat, *Pushkin* (New York, 1950), p. 13, quoted by R. Redfield, *The Primitive World and Its Transformations* (Ithaca, 1953), p. 40; for another modern example G. Bazin, *The Baroque* (Greenwich, Conn., 1968), p. 322.

CHAPTER 4

1. K. Hopkins in *Trade and the Ancient Economy*, ed. P. Garnsey et al. (Berkeley, 1983), p. xii, quoted with approval by J. F. Matthews, *Journal of Roman Studies* 74 (1984), p. 170.
2. M. I. Finley, *The Ancient Economy* (2d ed.; Berkeley, 1985), p. 98, doubts the figure often given of 6 to 8% as "normal return on investment in land," but this must be in the right range, though precision is impossible in view of factors that cannot be quantified accurately.
3. *Works and Days* 341; *Politics* 2. 3 1265b; see generally my *Economic and Social Growth of Early Greece*, pp. 150–51.
4. G. G. Busolt, *Griechische Staatskunde*, 1 (3d ed.; Munich, 1920), pp. 352–58.
5. Against M. Jameson, "Agriculture and Slavery in Classical Athens," *Classical Journal* 73 (1977), pp. 122–41, see the firm rebuttal by E. M. Wood, "Agricultural Slavery in Classical Athens," *American Journal of Ancient History* 8 (1983), pp. 1–47.
6. Finley, *The Ancient Economy*, p. 99, citing as an example the Buselos family (Davies, *Athenian Propertied Families*, no. 2921).
7. See the estimates in my *Economic and Social Growth*, p. 154.

8. Plutarch, *Pericles* 16.

9. M. I. Rostovtzeff, *A Large Estate in Egypt in the Third Century B. C.* (Madison, 1922); *Social and Economic History of the Hellenistic World* (Oxford, 1941), index *s. v..* Zenon.

10. I borrow the summary of Finley, *The Ancient Economy*, p. 116, based on Demosthenes 27. 9–11.

11. Bolkestein, *Economic Life in Greece's Golden Age*, pp. 63–65.

12. P. MacKendrick, *The Athenian Aristocracy 399 to 31 B. C.* (Cambridge, Mass., 1969), p. 8, dubiously seeks to link the orator to the Bouzyges family.

13. Plutarch, *Solon* 2, who goes on to observe that "some say he travelled to get experience and learning rather than make money," but points out that "the calling of a merchant was actually held in honor" in early Greece.

14. Colaeus and Sostratus: Herodotus 4. 152, 4. 52; M. Torelli, *Parola del Passato* 26 (1971), pp. 56ff.; A. W. Johnston, *Parola del Passato* 27 (1972), pp. 416–23.

15. *Odyssey* 8. 159–64. True calculation of "profit," however, was surely as difficult then as in nineteenth-century America; cf. A. D. Chandler, Jr., *The Visible Hand* (Cambridge, Mass., 1977), pp. 39, 397.

16. Hesiod, *Works and Days* 307; Solon fr. 1; Alcaeus fr. 360 (quoted also by Pindar in *Isthmian* 2. 9ff.).

17. P. A. Cartledge, "Trade and Politics Revisited: Archaic Greece," *Trade and the Ancient Economy*, pp. 1–15; *Ober, Mass and Elite*, p. 58.

18. Compare the emphasis on luxury trade in the sixteenth century after Christ: F. M. Braudel, *The Mediterranean and the Mediterranean World*, 1 (New York, 1972), pp. 441, 551.

19. See the specific discussion in my *Economic and Social Growth*, pp. 64–70.

20. J. F. Shepherd and G. M. Walton, *Shipping, Maritime Trade, and the Economic Development of North America* (Cambridge, 1972), p. 113 (woolens were 40% of all goods of British manufacture).

21. Demosthenes 34. 51; cf. G. M. Calhoun, *The Business Life of Ancient Athens* (Chicago, 1926), still a valuable study.

22. J. H. D'Arms, *Commerce and Social Standing in Ancient Rome* (Cambridge, Mass, 1981).

23. Davies, *Athenian Propertied Families*, p. 31; cf. Andocides' own oration 1. 137.

24. *Nicomachean Ethics* 4. 1 1122a, frowns on those who lend at extortionate interest to secure unjust profit.

25. Braudel, *Capitalism and Materialism*, p. 124; parallel attitudes can often be found, but H. I. Pleket, *Vestigia* 17 (1973), p. 38, properly observes that he is not preaching a sermon and so will not "censure this mentality."

26. F. Redlich, "De Praeda Militari: Looting and Booty, 1500–1815," *Vierteljahrschrift für Sozial-und Wirtschaftsgeschichte*, Supp. 39 (1956).

27. *Illustrated English Social History* (Penguin paperback), 1, pp. 67, 179; 2, pp. 153–56.

28. R. Meiggs and D. Lewis, *Selection of Greek Historical Inscriptions* (Oxford, 1969), no. 33; I have commented on Athenian population in *Birth of Athenian Democracy*, p. 33.

29. Demosthenes 50; cf. my *Influence of Sea Power on Ancient History* (New York, 1989), pp. 47–48.

30. Aristotle, *Constitution of Athenians* 50.

31. V. de Falco, *Demade Oratore* (2d ed.; Naples, 1954), p. 31.

32. Old Oligarch 1.

CHAPTER 5

1. Diogenes Laertius 9. 6.

2. There was a dim tradition that Pythagoras had been a gem cutter, a report generally dismissed by modern students; it accords ill in any case with his prominent political position at Croton.

3. F. Lasserre and A. Bonnard, *Archiloque: Fragments* (Paris, 1955), nos. 13, 93.

4. *Theogony* 27–28.

5. Diehl, fr. 10.

6. Mimnermus, fr. 6; Solon, frr. 22, 21. On the idea of truth in early Greece see my essay in *Parola del Passato* 23 (1968), pp. 348–59 (now in my *Essays*, pp. 163–74).

7. *Hecataei Fragmenta*, ed. G. Nenci (Florence, 1954), fr. 1.

8. C. M. Bowra, *Greek Lyric Poetry from Alcman to Simonides* (2d ed.; Oxford, 1961), pp. 168–71.

9. Thucydides 2. 37.

10. E. Derenne, *Les Procès d'impiété intentés aux philosophes à Athènes au Vme et au IVme siècles avant J.-C.* (Liège, 1930), remains a level-headed study. Even Euripides, who played no active political role, was charged with *asebeia* by Cleon (Satyrus, *Life of Euripides*, col. 10).

11. I. F. Stone, *The Trial of Socrates* (Boston, 1988), is not as novel as he suggested.

12. Cf. D. M. Schullian, *External Stimuli to Literary Production in Rome, 90–27 B. C.* (Diss. Chicago, 1932); an interesting early modern parallel, M. Biagioli, "Galileo the Emblem-Maker," *Isis* 81 (1990), pp. 230–55.

13. T. B. L. Webster, *Potter and Patron in Classical Athens* (London, 1972), p. 299; A. Burford, *Craftsmen in Greek and Roman Society* (London, 1972), c. 4, is explicit: "without patronage the craftsman starved" (p. 135).

14. Burford, *Craftsmen*, pp. 128–34.

15. A. Burford, *The Greek Temple Builders at Epidaurus* (Toronto, 1969), pp. 138–45, though she reacts too strongly against modern praises of Greek architects.

16. Vitruvius 7 praef.

17. J. J. Coulton, "Lifting in Early Greek Architecture," *Journal of Hellenic Studies* 94 (1974), pp. 1–19; see more generally his *Greek Architects at Work* (London, 1977).

18. *Inscriptiones Graecae* II no. 1668.

19. Studies of Greek architecture almost always limit themselves to discussing specific buildings; Burford, *Temple Builders at Epidaurus*, pp. 88–118, dissects more fully the building contracts.

20. R. Meiggs and D. Lewis, *Selection of Greek Historical Inscriptions* (Oxford, 1969), no. 44.

21. It might be noted that Nicosthenes, a prolific potter of the sixth century, designed his products to be sold in Etruria with Etruscan vase shapes and mythical scenes that could appeal to Etruscan nobles; cf. M. M. Eisman, "Attic Kyathos Production," *Archaeology* 28 (1975), pp. 76–83, and *American Journal of Archaeology* 74 (1970), p. 193. On the appearance of Aeneas-Anchises on export vases see J. Boardman, *Athenian Black Figure Vases* (London, 1974), p. 197.

22. R. M. Cook, *Greek Painted Pottery* (London, 1960), p. 258, who notes that a few such vases celebrate female beauties.

23. L. H. Schneider, "Zur sozial Bedeutung der Korai-Statuen," *Hamburger Beiträge zur Archäeologie*, Beiheft 2 (1972), unfortunately promises more than is given.

24. Burford, *Craftsmen*, pp. 125ff., is sagacious on this problem.

CHAPTER 6

1. *Odyssey* 11. 489–91.

2. *Politics* 7. 8 1328b, cf. 6. 8 1322b. In the Ancien Régime, protection of the established church was a principal responsibility of government; cf. G. Rudé, *Europe in the Eighteenth Century* (London, 1972), p. 103.

3. F. Sokolowski, *Lois sacrées des cités grecques* (Paris, 1969), no. 110; cf. the effort to exclude Cleomenes from the temple of

Athena on the Acropolis and the rule in Aristotle, *Politics* 7. 8 1329a, that only citizens can worship the gods.

4. A. J. Festugière, *Personal Religion among the Greeks* (Berkeley, 1954), p. 6.

5. Homer, *Epigrammata*, ed. D. B. Munro (Oxford, 1896), no. 14.

6. So too in Rome according to C. Koch, *Der römische Juppiter* (Frankfurt, 1937), and others the gods had an upper-class stamp, though this may be argued.

7. Xenophanes frr. 14, 30, and others.

8. *Works and Days* 217ff., 254–55.

9. Solon fr. 3.

10. J. Pollard, *Seers, Shrines and Sirens* (London, 1965), pp. 44–45; see generally H. W. Parke, *Festivals of the Athenians* (London, 1977), and for *polis* cults as a whole C. Sourvinou-Inwood, *The Greek City from Homer to Alexander*, pp. 295–322, and a companion paper promised there.

11. M. P. Nilsson, *Geschichte der griechischen Religion* 1 (2d ed.; Munich, 1955), p. 709, gives a comprehensive list.

12. J. H. Oliver, *The Athenian Expounders of the Sacred and Ancestral Law* (Baltimore, 1950), p. 17, puts in proper perspective the use of prophecies by Athenian aristocrats for political purposes; Ober, *Mass and Elite*, p. 57, is also skeptical.

13. Nilsson, p. 408.

14. Nilsson, p. 714.

15. Nilsson, p. 710.

16. Aristotle, *Constitution of the Athenians* 21. 6.

17. Cf. my essay, "Religion and Patriotism in Fifth-century Athens," *Panathenaia*, ed. T. E. Gregory and A. J. Podlecki (Lawrence, Kansas, 1979), pp. 11–26.

18. *Supplementum Epigraphicum Graecum* 9. 1 (Leiden, 1938), no. 72, on the rules at Cyrene in the early fourth century.

19. Pausanias 1. 17. 1, 1. 24. 3, though, as I noted in my essay on religion and patriotism, this remark was probably true only in a formal sense, much as papal Rome could be described in the late eighteenth century.

CHAPTER 7

1. P. MacKendrick, *The Athenian Aristocracy 399 to 31 B. C.* (Cambridge, Mass., 1969), gives more than sufficient detail about the role of noble *gennetai*.

2. See generally M. I. Rostovtzeff, *Social and Economic History of the Hellenistic World* (Oxford, 1941), e. g., pp. 1116–26, 1304–05.

3. Plutarch, *Themistocles* 32. 4; *Inscriptiones Graecae* II. 2, no. 2291a.

4. Horace, *Epistles* 2. 1. 156, "Graecia capta ferum victorem cepit."

5. T. Mommsen, *History of Rome*, Book II, c. 8; unfortunately Appian, *Samnite Wars* 7, reports that Postumius committed barbarisms (so too Dionysius of Halicarnassus 19. 5).

6. My *Beginnings of Imperial Rome* (Ann Arbor, 1980), pp. 49–51.

7. W. H. Gross, "Zum sogennanten Brutus," *Hellenismus in Mittelitalien*, ed. P. Zanker (Göttingen, 1976), pp. 564–75, opts for an Augustan date; M. Torelli, *Roma mediorepubblicana* ed. F. Coarelli (Rome, 1973), p. 31, on the other hand argues for about 340 B.C., though this may be too early.

8. See generally A. Wardman, *Rome's Debt to Greece* (New York, 1977), which concentrates on the era from Cicero to the second century after Christ; and from the Greek point of view A. Momigliano, *Alien Wisdom* (Cambridge, 1976).

9. *Civilization and the Caesars: The Intellectual Revolution in the Roman Empire* (Ithaca, 1954).

10. In the following summary I am indebted especially to W. L. Wiley, *The Gentleman of Renaissance France* (Cambridge, Mass., 1954), written with wit and good judgment, and also to E. Barker, *Traditions of Civility* (Cambridge, 1948).

11. Wiley, p. 25.

12. Barker, p. 143.

13. I have found most useful A. Goodwin, ed., *The European*

Nobility in the Eighteenth Century (London, 1953), which surveys ten European aristocracies, and J. B. Labatut, *Les noblesses europeénes de la fin du XVe siècle à la fin du XVIIIe siècle* (Paris, 1978). Recently a number of English scholars have found aristocracy a fascinating subject, as J. Powis, *Aristocracy* (Oxford, 1984), and S. Winchester, *Their Noble Lordships* (London, 1981), whose hostility to nobility leads him to conclude (p. 305) that England must emulate Japan "to win the admiration of the Bangladeshi and the Venezuelan, the Kenyan and the Michigander"—an odd combination indeed. The tombstone has recently been erected by D. Cannadine, *The Decline and Fall of the British Aristocracy* (New Haven, 1990).

14. Machiavelli, *Discorsi* 1. 55. 7.

15. A. Trollope, *Ralph the Heir*, c. 16 ad fin.

16. D. M. Kennedy, *Atlantic*, November 1990, p. 164. The discussions of the New England ethic by Perry Miller and others are well known; not so evidently relevant is W. J. Cash, *The Mind of the South* (New York, 1941), though his remarks on the preservation of hierarchy (p. 253) could be applied *ipsissimis verbis* to the political practices of Greek aristocracies in their heyday.

Bibliography

SOURCES

For the texts of the epics I have relied on the Oxford editions;
for Hesiod, the new edition by M. L. West (Oxford, 1978),
and for translation that of H. G. Evelyn-White (Loeb Classical
Library). Fragments of the early poets are given in the nu-
meration of E. Diehl's edition (3 vols.; 3d ed., Leipzig, 1952–
55) save for Archilochus, cited from F. Lasserre and A. Bonnard (Paris, 1958), and for Sappho and Alcaeus, E. Lobel
and D. Page (Oxford, 1955). Translations of Herodotus and
Thucydides are usually from the Penguin volumes of A. de

Selincourt and Rex Warner; texts are those of the Oxford editions. Aristotle's works are cited by the running heads in the Teubner texts; the translation of the *Politics* is that of E. Barker. Inscriptions are given as far as possible from R. Meiggs and D. Lewis (Oxford, 1969).

COLLECTED ESSAYS

The Craft of the Ancient Historian: Essays in Honor of Chester G. Starr, ed. J. W. Eadie and J. Ober (Lanham, Md., 1985).
The Greek City from Homer to Alexander, ed. O. Murray and S. Price (New York, 1990).
The Greek Renaissance of the Eighth Century B. C., ed. R. Hägg (Stockholm, 1983).
C. G. Starr, *Essays on Ancient History*, ed. A. Ferrill and T. Kelly (Leiden, 1979).

MODERN WORKS

The following list is rigorously selective and brief, a reflection of the fact that Greek aristocracy has not received much attention of late.

A. W. H. Adkins, *Merit and Responsibility* (Oxford, 1960).
A. W. H. Adkins, *Moral Values and Political Behaviour in Ancient Greece* (London, 1972).
M. T. W. Arnheim, *Aristocracy in Greek Society* (New York, 1977).
G. Busolt, *Griechische Staatskunde*, 2 vol. (3d ed.; Munich, 1920–26).
J. K. Davies, *Athenian Propertied Families 600–300 B. C.* (Oxford, 1971).

W. Donlan, *The Aristocratic Ideal in Archaic Greece* (Lawrence, Kansas, 1986).

V. Ehrenberg, *The Greek State* (Norton paperback, 1964).

M. I. Finley, *The Ancient Economy* (Berkeley, 1973).

W. G. Forrest, *The Emergence of Greek Democracy* (London, 1966).

F. Gschnitzer, *Griechische Sozialgeschichte von der mykenischen bis zum Ausgang der klassischen Zeit* (Wiesbaden, 1981).

P. MacKendrick, *The Athenian Aristocracy 399 to 31 B. C.* (Cambridge, Mass., 1969).

J. Ober, *Mass and Elite in Democratic Athens* (Princeton, 1989).

M. Ostwald, *Nomos and the Beginnings of the Athenian Democracy* (Oxford, 1969).

C. G. Starr, *Individual and Community: The Rise of the Polis 800–500 B. C.* (New York, 1986).

C. G. Starr, *The Economic and Social Growth of Early Greece 800–500 B. C.* (New York, 1977).

L. Whibley, *Greek Oligarchies: Their Character and Organisation* (London, 1896).

R. F. Willetts, *Aristocratic Society in Ancient Crete* (London, 1953).

Index